Profitability
and
Systematic
Trading

Founded in 1807, John Wiley & Sons is the oldest independent publishing company in the United States. With offices in North America, Europe, Australia and Asia, Wiley is globally committed to developing and marketing print and electronic products and services for our customers' professional and personal knowledge and understanding.

The Wiley Trading series features books by traders who have survived the market's ever changing temperament and have prospered—some by reinventing systems, others by getting back to basics. Whether a novice trader, professional or somewhere in-between, these books will provide the advice and strategies needed to prosper today and well into the future.

For a list of available titles, visit our Web site at www.WileyFinance.com.

Profitability and Systematic Trading

MICHAEL HARRIS

WILEY

John Wiley & Sons, Inc.

Published by John Wiley & Sons, Inc., Hoboken, New Jersey.
Published simultaneously in Canada.

For general information on our other products and services or for technical support, please contact our Customer Care Department within the United States at (800) 762-2974, outside the United States at (317) 572-3993 or fax (317) 572-4002.

Wiley also publishes its books in a variety of electronic formats. Some content that appears in print may not be available in electronic books. For more information about Wiley products, visit our web site at www.wiley.com.

Library of Congress Cataloging-in-Publication Data:

Harris, Michael, 1958–
    Profitability and systematic trading : a quantitative approach to profitability, risk, and money management / Michael Harris.
        p. cm. – (Wiley trading series)
    Includes bibliographical references and index.
    ISBN 978-0-470-22908-8 (cloth)
    1. Stock price forecasting.   2. Investment analysis.   3. Speculation.   I. Title.
    HG4637.H3725   2008
    332.63′228–dc22

                                                                    2007050508

Printed in the United States of America.

10 9 8 7 6 5 4 3 2 1

To Emmy, Christine and Katherine

Contents

Preface

The rapid technological progress in information processing technology is changing every aspect of our lives. The financial markets cannot escape this technological impact. Investing and trading has shifted from the old paradigm of watching quote screens, calling a broker to place an order, and then waiting for a call with the order fill, to a new paradigm, based on real-time chart displays, electronic screen trading, and direct market access with fast executions.

Equally rapid are the advancements in the quantity and quality of information available to investors and traders as well as in the software applications for processing and analyzing it. Despite all the advancements made, traders and investors are still faced with the same old dilemma: *buy, sell, or hold?*

One could also assert that the numerous technological advancements, the abundance of information, and improved means of processing have increased the complexity and the difficulty of trading for a profit rather than making the life of traders easier. This assertion is partly due to the fact that markets have become more efficient while opportunities are becoming scarce and increasingly difficult to identify. More and more, traders report failures of trading systems developed not too long ago, which had produced in the past excellent back testing and actual trading records. There are a few possible causes for these failures: One cause can be found in the widespread use or popularization (if I may call it that) of technical analysis—that is, a method of evaluating market action that relies primarily on the analysis of price and volume. Some believe that traders using technical methods no longer have a competitive advantage. Others believe that the failures are due to the ability of some market participants to affect price direction and thus generate false technical signals followed by sudden price reversals. I will not attempt to discuss or investigate such claims here, but there may be some truth hidden in them.

My view is that most trading systems failures are due to a wrong application of system development and risk management principles. Traders know that the most important function of a trading system is the timing of entry and exit signals. But that is exactly where most technical analysis methods have deficiencies. This deficiency arises because of the time lag between price action and the reaction of technical analysis methods. Specifically, the majority of technical analysis indicators lag price movement because they consider only past prices in their calculations, and this allows fast traders to capitalize on this deficiency, position themselves in the market early, and then profit by satisfying the demand created by technical traders whose systems respond too late. Thus, use of appropriate models and their careful analysis is of paramount importance to the success of a technical trader trying to survive in a highly competitive trading game. This success depends on the development and application of models that offer a competitive advantage, combined with the use of risk and money management methods that minimize the risk of ruin while maximizing returns. This is the name of the game in a nutshell, and this book will explore this game in depth.

RATIONALE AND STRUCTURE OF THE BOOK

This book is divided into three sections. Part I, "Foundations," provides the essential knowledge a trader must posses before attempting to develop winning trading methodologies. At the same time, this part attempts to confront some popular misconceptions about the markets. Chapter 1 presents an account of the market based on the notion of the term *market participants*, which is more appropriate for technical traders. Chapter 2 discusses the relationship between trading and the zero-sum game; while Chapter 3 investigates the different time frames and methods of analysis used by traders.

Part II, "Profitability and Risk," offers a quantitative assessment of profitability and risk and money management. In my opinion, a mastery of these concepts is required before a trader can proceed with the development of trading systems. Specifically, an understanding of the limitations imposed by profitability requirements on trading system design, and of the restrictions that prudent risk and money management place on capital requirements, are of fundamental importance for success. In Chapter 4, the profitability rule and its implications in the development of trading systems are discussed. Chapter 5 focuses on risk and money management, In particular, it focuses on determining the minimum starting capital required for trading a system and calculating position sizing.

Part III, "Systematic Trading," focuses on the process of trading system development. Going through this process is essential for every systematic trader and success depends greatly on the trader's understanding of the intricate details involved and the hidden traps. In Chapter 6, I discuss the analysis of trading systems and expose some pitfalls of back testing. In Chapter 7, I offer an introduction to the process of the synthesis of trading systems and present some specific examples that illustrate this powerful methodology of trading system development.

While reading these chapters, you may be surprised by the lack of charts and figures in this trading book. I am not in favor of trading methodologies that rely on visual chart analysis. Charts can impose illusions on the human mind, most often by reflecting what one wishes to see in them. Therefore, I tried to limit the number of chart examples in the book to those absolutely necessary to illustrate the points made. On the other hand, there is no need for someone to buy a book just to look at chart examples! A good book must contain valuable information for the reader in exchange for the price paid for it. By overwhelming the reader with charts and indicators plotted on them and by offering just another subjective interpretation of price behavior, there is no valuable contribution made. Fancy charts are easily accessible nowadays by anyone with a personal computer and on-line access. In order to stay profitable, one must go beyond subjective interpretations of price behavior and visual chart analysis. Traders who are determined to be successful need to apply a more rigorous and in-depth approach leading to systematic trading. This is what the material in the book aims to accomplish by setting the foundations for the achievement of this difficult task.

WHY YOU SHOULD READ THIS BOOK

The feedback I have received from traders all over the world who have read my first two books has motivated me to write this one. There is no point in writing a book unless it offers value to the reader. This is exactly the purpose of this book. In *Profitability and Systematic Trading*, I expose the reader to a few very important concepts I have worked on during my 20 years of research and development on the subject. For example, the concept of synthesis of trading systems is one that I consider a novel approach that may hold the key to the future of trading system development. I strongly recommend that the reader go through the material starting from Part I, where I rebut some misconceptions people have about the markets. Common misconceptions have a negative impact on any efforts to profit from trading or investing, yet they are so widespread that they have become "market folklore." I also strongly recommend following the derivation of the profitability rule in Part II and reading the chapter on risk and money management carefully. My experience is that even in the case that one is not planning to develop advanced trading systems using analysis or the most advanced and novel method of synthesis given in Part III, the information in parts I and II can serve as a guide to understanding the realities of trading and investing.

Acknowledgments

I would like to thank Mrs. Kelly O'Connor, development editor at John Wiley & Sons, for her invaluable professional help and advice in editing the manuscript.

About the Author

M ichael Harris started developing mechanical trading systems in the late 1980s while working for Wall Street firms. He has been an active trader since 1989. He is the author of the best sellers *Short-term Trading with Price Patterns* (1999) and *Stock Trading Techniques with Price Patterns* (2000), and has written many articles for popular trading journals as an invited author. He is also the developer of the highly acclaimed trading software APS Automatic Pattern Search, which finds trading systems automatically based on high-level performance criteria, and of the p-indicator, which is a new technical analysis indicator based on price patterns.

Michael is currently the president of Tradingpatterns.com, a company he established in 1999 that specializes in the development of advanced pattern recognition software for position and swing traders. He is also the director of Harrison Investments, Inc., a fund management and financial consulting firm for offshore institutional investors and hedge funds.

Michael Harris holds a Bachelor degree in Mechanical Engineering (Magna Cum Laude, SUNY at Buffalo, 1981) and two Master degrees, one in Systems Engineering (SUNY at Buffalo, 1983) and another in Operations Research (Columbia University, 1988). He has worked in the past for Bell Laboratories and several Wall Street firms.

Disclaimer

H ypothetical or simulated performance results have certain inherent limitations. Unlike an actual performance record, simulated results do not represent actual trading. Also, since the trades have not been executed, the results may be under- or overcompensated for the impact, if any, of certain market factors, such as lack of liquidity. Simulated trading programs in general are subject to the fact that they are designed with the benefit of hindsight. No representation is being made that any account will or is likely to achieve profits or losses similar to those shown.

The trading methods, systems, and patterns included in this book are for educational purposes only and none is recommended. Past results are not necessarily indicative of future results and, therefore, it should not be assumed that the use of any of the methods or techniques presented would result in trading profits. This is not a solicitation of any order to buy or sell. Trading stocks, futures, options on stocks or futures, or forex involves substantial financial risks and may result in total loss of capital.

PART I

Foundations

Every trader who desires to be profitable must have a clear under-standing of the operational structure of the market and in a way that is compatible with trading objectives and requirements. Becoming successful in dealing with the realities of technical trading and investing requires approaching markets from the right perspective. Adopting the appropriate account of the market described in detail in Chapter 1 is of fundamental importance to success.

Trading is mostly a zero-sum game; this is the subject of Chapter 2. Traders often fail to realize this fact because they align themselves with wrong perceptions of what markets really are and how they operate. It is very important that traders understand what are the implications of the zero-sum game nature of the markets for their efforts to make a profit.

The different methodologies used in trading and the different time frames involved are probably the most fundamental knowledge that traders must have before risking any money. In Chapter 3, the differences between technical and fundamental analysis are discussed, as well as, the different time frames used in trading.

Understanding what markets are all about, facing the reality of the zero-sum game, and knowing the trading methods and time frames involved, all from the perspective of systematic trading and investing, is of fundamental importance and serves as a foundation for the development of profitable trading methodologies.

CHAPTER 1

The Market

Some of the problems that traders face are due to the misleading concept that they have about what the word *market* means. Novice traders often risk their life savings without understanding the market structure and market dynamics. Many traders do not spend enough time educating themselves before they get involved in such a dynamic endeavor.

In this chapter, I provide the most relevant and realistic account of markets from the perspective of systematic traders and investors. I believe it is necessary for traders to understand this philosophy so that they can better understand how to operate within the market. I also discuss the characteristics of the different trading markets. A proper market account can also make a difference in the selection of a specific market to concentrate in. Although the final selection depends on many factors, at the end of this chapter I attempt to clarify some aspects of the markets that often influence the selection process.

A TRADER'S PERSPECTIVE

News reporters, traders, investors, and even laymen are constantly using the word *market*. Some phrases that are often heard or read as part of reports in electronic and print media are "the market fell today," "the market bounced off its recent lows," and "the market was hit by waves of selling." Moreover, some typical statements made by traders are "the market went against me," "the market took my stops," or "the market was volatile." The

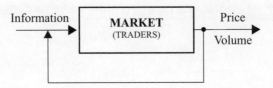

FIGURE 1.1 Fundamental account of the market.

phrases just quoted and a host of others containing the word *market* all
have something in common: They are potentially misleading or even false
statements because the market is not some real entity, which acts or is
acted upon. Instead, the market is made up of all those who participate in
it, called the *market participants*. Any attempt to assign a special or absolute quality to the word *market*, other than the fact that it is the collection
of its participants, is a distortion of reality and may eventually lead to false
trading or investing decisions.

Figure 1.1 illustrates the fundamental account of the market as a collection of traders and investors participating in all sorts of transactions.
The input to the market is information, which drives the decision processes
of its participants. The output of the market is the price of the financial instruments traded and volume. Price and volume, current and historical, are
also part of the information that causes participants to act, especially technical traders. As a matter of fact, a good part of technical trading is based
solely on the analysis of price and volume historical data series.

The account of the market just presented is valid at every time period,
whether it is a day, a week, a month, five minutes, or even at every price
tick. It is the most fundamental account from a systems input–output perspective and one that is especially useful to technical traders and investors.

Whether the market can be defined only in terms of its participants or
as an entity with an absolute existence above and beyond its participants
is a much more complicated issue than it first seems. However, what matters most from the point of view of trading and investing is the operational
structure of the market from a practical perspective rather than its onto-
logical status.

The proper account of the market provided here is based on the fact
that markets cannot exist at all unless traders and investors participate.
Therefore, defining a market in terms of its participants is well founded.
Anything else above and beyond this empirical account is an irrelevant or
even dangerous perspective for a trader or investor to have. This is because, even if it is the case and markets are something more than their
participants, there is no way to empirically determine the resulting properties of such an entity and use the knowledge in trading methodologies
with quantifiable content. On the contrary, any abstract views, or even

postulations, can alienate one from the reality of markets and eventually lead to an emotive approach to trading and investing with disastrous consequences.

The collective actions of the participating traders and investors in a market determine the direction of prices, depending on the liquidity added or subtracted in association with the given price level. More importantly, the operational structure of markets is such that for every buyer there must be a seller. When buyers concede to higher sell offers, prices rise. On the other hand, when sellers concede to lower buy offers, prices drop. The reasons for this pattern of price behavior are not important for the purpose of this analysis; however, it is important to be aware of this relationship. Even if there are some other causal connections, real or ethereal, affecting price behavior and direction, prices move because of the actions of market participants. In other words, there are no magical transactions occurring in the market and every transaction involves a real buyer and a real seller. It is eventually just the participants' actions that determine price and volume.

Based on this well-defined operational structure of the market, a prospective trader or investor must recognize that the market is just a collection of active traders and investors, the people who participate in it, people just like him. With this understanding of the meaning of the word *market*, a better choice in place of the phrase "the market fell today" is "sellers conceded to lower buy offers today." Likewise, "the market bounced off its recent lows" should be interpreted as "buy offers bounced to higher levels from their recent lows"; and "the market was hit by waves of selling" may be better put as "sellers conceded to waves of lower buy offers."

Assigning to the word *market* its proper meaning while rejecting emotive, metaphysical, and absurd notions that view the market as an entity that exists above and beyond its own participants, are very important first steps to take for every trader and investor who desires to be a winner. Then, "the market went against me" means "other traders took an opposite view to the one I took and were right." Similarly, "the market took my stops" means that "other traders took my buy/sell offer" and "the market was volatile" simply means, "prices were volatile." Thus, whenever a trader hears the word *market*, he must try to visualize other traders just like him, from an office or a home or in a trading pit, all attempting to forecast what the future price direction will be with the objective to profit from it. Those who can either influence the actions of other traders using their financial power or forecast future price direction with a high rate of success using their wisdom are the ones who ultimately win. Thinking in terms of "me against the market" is a loser's attitude. Every trader or investor is just a participant in the market, and his or her actions are part of the collective activity the set defines.

There are two basic qualities that contribute most to trading profitability: power and wisdom. If a trader is powerful enough he can profit by positioning in the market at attractive price levels and then enticing other traders to act while satisfying their demand or absorbing their supply, depending on the direction of prices. If a trader is wise enough she can achieve high profitability from forecasting the future direction of prices, influenced by the collective actions of other participants, and accomplish that by analyzing information in ingenious ways, ultimately predicting how others will act based on that information. Unless there is power or wisdom involved, there is no hope for anyone to succeed and any such participant lacking both of these prerequisites will eventually end up transferring his or her wealth to other more qualified traders.

The remaining part of this chapter deals primarily with a comparison of futures, equity, and forex trading. Any reference to the word *market* is simply a reference to the collection of its participants—retail and professional traders, specialists, market makers, institutional traders, and so on. The same holds true for the remaining part of the book.

FUTURES, EQUITY, AND FOREX MARKETS

The majority of technical traders are participants in the equity, futures, or foreign exchange (forex) markets. There are several other very liquid markets—such as fixed income securities, interest rate swaps, and collateral mortgage obligations—that are mostly at the institutional level and are not suitable to retail traders because participation requires establishing credit lines with financial institutions.

Retail traders and small-to-medium-sized funds participate in these three most popular markets and use brokers to place their orders. Prior to the early 1990s, the bulk of retail trading volume was done in the commodity futures markets. The bull stock market of the late 1990s was the main reason for the dramatic increase in the number of equity traders. This coincided in time with an explosive growth in the field of information technology and use of the World Wide Web. The new technology contributed to the emergence of online equity brokers, but similar applications in futures and forex retail trading lagged behind mainly due to technical and regulatory issues.

During the 1990s, most of the commodity futures exchanges were still operating based on open-outcry pit trading, while forex trading was an unregulated institutional market dominated by large banks. After the rapid market decline, which followed the bull stock market of the late 1990s, there was a resumption of interest in retail futures trading. The introduction of 24-hour electronic screen trading in several futures markets and the addition of popular products like the S&P 500 and Dow Jones Industrials mini-sized futures contracts contributed to a steady influx of new retail traders. That further led to an increasing number of futures brokerages offering online order placement. At the same time, forex market makers offering online order placement and execution to individual retail traders started to emerge. As the liquidity and momentum of the equity markets subsided, those introduced to trading and technical analysis through the equity markets started to switch to futures and forex markets in search of opportunities to apply their skills and hopefully profit from them.

Traders who plan to develop systematic trading methodologies must understand the characteristics of each popular market they intend to work within. Market-specific characteristics often impose constraints on the development of a trading methodology. For example, intraday and short-term traders must be especially aware of any daily limits imposed on price moves. And forex and futures traders must understand how the margin works and its effects on trading system designs and risk and money management. In the following section, important characteristics of the most popular trading markets are presented in more detail.

Futures Markets

Futures markets are organized financial exchanges where participants can trade standardized futures contracts. Futures markets offer moderate to high liquidity at moderate to low commission costs. These markets are under strict regulation and supervision, and there is a time and sales report available to all participants. Such a report is extremely valuable because traders can always verify broker fills using the exchange records. Futures markets are structured to guarantee smooth execution of orders and the elimination of counterparty credit risk by imposing sufficient margin requirements. Thus, traders can safely ignore operational and counterparty risk–related issues and focus on their methodology and analysis, whether fundamental or technical.

A few important characteristics of futures markets that play an important role in the development of systematic trading methodologies are:

Leverage: The most attractive feature of futures markets, one that highly appeals to retail traders and fund managers, is the high leverage. The low margin requirements per contract allow leveraging of positions, but this can work favorably if the forecast of the future price direction turns out to be right or against the trader if it turns out to be wrong. Futures contracts never default or become worthless, but high leverage can have an equivalent effect on a trader's account.

Due to the high leverage, as discussed in Chapter 5, prudent risk and money management must be an integral part of every systematic futures trading system; otherwise the risk of ruin becomes very high.

Daily price limits: Most futures contracts have daily price limits. A daily limit is the maximum price advance from the previous day's settlement price permitted during the trading session. In some futures contracts, the daily limit may change during the trading session based on a predefined time schedule set by the exchange. Similar rules apply to stock indexes but, in comparison, forex markets never lock limit up or down because they are not regulated by any exchange. This is the reason currency futures do not have daily limits. The same is true with most interest rate, metals, and index futures contracts, because their spot commodities do not have any daily limits imposed on them. Grain and Oilseed and Livestock futures all have daily limits imposed.

Although stock index price limits were put in place to protect markets from excessive daily drops, like the stock market crash of 1987, for example, limits in general can work either for or against a trader.

If an exchange does not close trading, then a general rule is that only selling is allowed when the price of a futures contract locks limit up, and only buying is allowed when the price locks limit down. If a trader is caught short in a locked limit up market, she cannot buy contracts to offset her open position. The same holds for long position holders in a locked limit down market, where no selling is allowed. In the event that prices open locked, limit up or down, in consecutive trading sessions, a trader can be faced with a financial disaster that is beyond her control if there is no alternative way of hedging her position.

Lumber futures, as an example, went through a series of locked limit up trading sessions in early 1993, as shown in Figure 1.2. There were at least 10 trading sessions that remained locked limit up from the open of the trading session starting on January 25, 1993. The rally in lumber prices continued to mid-March of the same year with scattered locked limit up trading sessions.

Anyone caught net short Lumber futures on January 25, 1993, could not buy contracts to close open positions until around February 8. Unable to do anything, they watched their trading account equity plummet and even go into the red. On the other hand, those who were long made windfall profits. Some of the traders who were caught short lumber futures during the specific streak of locked limit up sessions ended up losing a fortune. The best way for technical traders to

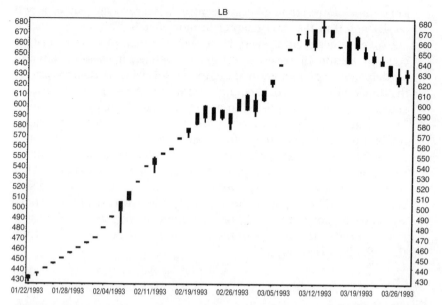

FIGURE 1.2 Limit up trading sessions in lumber futures.
Source: APS Automatic Pattern Search.

avoid such rare situations is either by staying away from markets that have daily limits imposed and offer no alternative way out, or by taking small and easily manageable risk in proportion to their trading capital.

Bear markets: Futures have bear markets but it is not clear how this affects the profitability of systematic technical trading. Traders can go long or short futures with the same ease and speed. It has been observed, however, that during bear markets liquidity decreases. It appears, based on experience, that technical trading methods tend to be more effective during bull markets than bear markets (and much less effective during sideways-moving or fluctuating markets). This is a bit paradoxical at first glance since the notion of rising or falling prices is a matter of convention from the point of view of the analysis of price charts. However, it seems that bear markets are less technically driven than bull markets, and this is the fundamental reason for the decrease in the effectiveness of systematic trading methodologies during falling markets. Whereas greed and technical trading dominate a bull market, fear and panic dominate a bear market. Equity trading also suffers from the same effects but this is not the case with forex trading, because with currencies there is no such thing as a bear market.

Zero-sum game: Trading futures contracts is a zero-sum game, as will be discussed in the next chapter in more detail. This means that at any given time, even at every price tick, the sum of profits must be equal to the sum of losses. At the end of each trading session, after all participants' accounts are marked-to-market using settlement prices, the total credit posted to accounts with winning open positions always equals the total debit posted to accounts with losing open positions. This means that for a trader to profit in futures trading, some other trader must lose. Since there are no speculators willing to lose money in the futures markets, profitable trading requires a means of making the right predictions about price direction. This means among other things outsmarting or overpowering other traders by forecasting successfully or affecting price direction for one's own advantage. Those who have no power to affect price direction can rely only on their wisdom to predict the actions of the other participants and benefit from the resulting price moves.

Equity Markets

As in the case of futures markets, similar considerations also hold for equity markets regarding the regulated structure of exchanges, moderate to high liquidity, low commissions, and transaction report availability. A few important characteristics of the equity markets that often play an important role in the development of systematic trading methodologies are:

Liquidity, leverage, and bear markets: Some equity markets, such as the *over the counter (OTC) market*, may not provide enough liquidity and are not suitable for technical systematic trading. Most component stocks of the S&P 500 and NASDAQ 100 indexes are very liquid and popular to trade. So are some of the recently developed *exchange traded funds*, such as the QQQQ and SPY. However, position leveraging via the use of margin is not as attractive a feature as it is in the case of futures and forex trading. Margin requirements are high, short positions can be taken only in selected issues that fulfill certain criteria, and there is extra cost and increased risk involved. Equity markets may exhibit protracted bear markets, where the inability to short some issues virtually diminishes the potential to profit from such moves. But more importantly, short-covering periods in bear markets are frequent and dominated by violent price moves. This reality of equity markets forces many traders to chase short-term upward price reversals that occur in bear markets, which demands a timing accuracy that is very difficult to get using technical analysis methods.

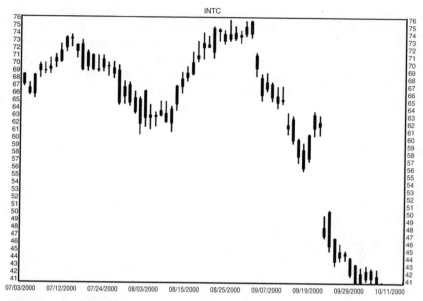

FIGURE 1.3 Example of an opening gap in INTC stock.
Source: APS Automatic Pattern Search.

Equity trading can be halted: The actions of market makers and specialists can affect the direction of the price of a stock during periods of low liquidity. Furthermore, trading of a stock can be halted at any time and without prior warning, and when trading resumes the price may gap up or down significantly, which is something that never occurs in futures or forex markets. The same holds true when unexpected earnings reports are released or other surprising news about a listed company hits the wire. As an example, the stock of Intel Corp. (INTC) plummeted more than $15 on the open of September 21, 2000 after a disappointing earnings report was released the previous evening, as shown in the chart in Figure 1.3. The risks from such random events are high and can erase profits accumulated over extended periods of trading activity. However, one must also realize that there are those who benefit from such random events—in the specific example just mentioned, short-sellers, call option writers, and put option holders, to name a few—but a systematic approach to take advantage of such random events is, of course, impossible to devise.

Not always a zero-sum game: In equity markets there are participants who may be willing to lose, such as companies repurchasing their stock, giving an opportunity for traders to profit from a rise in their stock price. The reverse effect that works against traders is when company insiders sell because they need for various reasons to reduce their stake in a company. These insiders profit at the expense of traders and investors. Also, equity trading is not always a zero-sum game during certain periods due to creation or destruction of wealth. These issues will be further discussed in the next chapter, which deals with zero-sum games.

Forex Markets

Forex markets facilitate over-the-counter transactions of one currency for another. Unlike futures and equity markets, these markets have no central clearance. Retail forex trading offers very high leverage (up to 200:1), very high liquidity, 24-hour trading, and a market that is difficult for participants to manipulate, although that seems to be easy to do in the short-term for politicians, central bank officials, and some special-interest groups. Trading currencies is by and large a zero-sum game, and there are no bear markets because quoted currency prices are exchange rates between pairs and a rise in the value of a currency makes sense only in reference to the drop in value of another currency. More than 75 percent of the daily volume of forex markets is speculative. As such, there is a lot of competition and effort made by its participants to redistribute wealth.

Some important aspects of forex trading that can greatly impact profitability are:

No commission-free trading: There is a misconception, or maybe misinformation, that commission-free forex trading is possible. Online forex brokers that advertise zero commission rates do this because they need to attract customers in order to pool enough accounts together so they can efficiently and profitably act as market makers. Traders end up paying commissions in the form of wide bid–ask spreads. In most cases, commissions are added to the order fill price, and when a trader opens a new position it always starts with an open loss. Forex market makers can do this because the market is self-regulated and transactions are over-the-counter.

No times and sales report: Note that there is no time and sales report available for the forex market as a whole. Price quotes that one trader sees on his computer screen that is linked to one market maker data feed can slightly vary from those another trader sees on her screen that is linked to another market maker data feed. Thus, a limit order placed at a specific price level maybe executed by one market maker but not by another because the specific price level was never reached.

Retail disadvantage: Individuals trading from home or office cannot compete on a level playing field with professional forex traders based at bank dealing rooms and large financial institutions and profit from their losses in an intraday or even short-term time frame. Those professional traders have timely access to information about order flow and high-quality market analysis that enables them to always have a competitive advantage over individual traders.

Currencies trend: Due to the fact that currency prices tend to form protracted trends, a retail trader can accumulate profits using trend-following techniques provided there is the necessary skill and discipline in place, as will be further discussed in Chapter 3.

An example of two protracted price trends in the EUR/USD currency pair is shown in Figure 1.4. Prices trended down during 1999 and 2000 and then went in an uptrend in early 2002. Sideways markets can last for years, as shown in the daily chart of the GBP/USD pair in Figure 1.5. In this case, for a period of two years, from mid-2000 to mid-2002, GBP/USD prices fluctuated in the narrow range of 1.4000 to 1.5000. Only highly skilled and experienced traders can profit during extended periods of sideways-moving prices in a tight range, and this is always done at the expense of unskilled and inexperienced ones. But even during trending markets, high volatility can make the task of following a trend very difficult; this will be discussed in Chapter 3 in more detail.

Mostly a zero-sum game: Although forex trading is a zero-sum game, there are certain very rare occasions when some participants may be willing to lose. This, however, does not change the zero-sum nature of forex trading.

An example of such participants are central banks that either intervene in the currency markets in order to stabilize currency exchange rates or slow down the rapid evaluation or devaluation of a currency. Although it is not very clear whether central banks are net losers or winners over longer time periods (not that it really matters), over the short term they may be willing to inject substantial sums into the forex market in order to stabilize currency exchange rates within a target band. Central bank intervention cannot change the longer-term trend of currency exchange rates that is dictated by macroeconomic factors, but any intervention on their part presents traders with an opportunity to profit at their expense. Interventions always come, or are supposed to come, as a "surprise," but this is in regard to only the specific price levels and the timing. Experienced forex traders can anticipate interventions and can make fortunes if they are correct in timing them. Central banks act like bluffers in a poker game during periods of

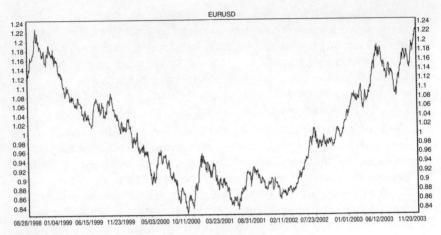

FIGURE 1.4   Example of a trending currency pair.
Source: APS Automatic Pattern Search.

FIGURE 1.5   Example of a sideways market in a currency pair.
Source: APS Automatic Pattern Search.

pending intervention and often let prices rally in the opposite direction from the one they target in order to shake out speculators. An experienced trader with a good "feel" of the market can profit from such moves, but such activity has little connection to systematic technical trading and it is fundamentally a game of chance carrying very high risk.

WHICH MARKET SHOULD I TRADE IN?

The answer to the question regarding which of the three markets, futures, equity, or forex, is most suitable to systematic technical trading can be given on a case-to-case basis, and only after considering which market(s) a trader understands best and feels most comfortable with. All three major trading markets offer opportunities, but also involve risk of total loss of capital. The most important aspect of trading is not which market one chooses to trade but the effectiveness of the methods used in generating market entry and exit signals and applying risk and money management.

One important factor in selecting a market to trade in is experience. Novice traders often concentrate on a single market, but experienced traders will trade anything that presents an opportunity to make a profit. Trading forex is a 24-hour job, and anyone who has been involved with it knows that one can easily lose a night's sleep if open positions are kept overnight. It's hard for a trader with an open position to relax when he knows that there is trading activity in a market, but intraday traders can also get anxious if they feel they are missing opportunities while they are asleep. Equity and futures markets are moving toward a 24-hour market operation structure in order to get a piece of the forex action, especially as trading becomes a global activity with traditionally socialist economies and China adopting capitalism. Eventually, all markets will be based on screen trading, and open outcry will be abolished.

A transition to 24-hour screen trading poses many challenges to traders but also increased opportunity for profit. One factor that is slowing down the conversion to a global, 24-hour, all-electronic trading market is the time difference in the operation of local banks and clearing members. Automation technology and the World Wide Web are rapidly changing that as banks and clearing members are linking their databases and automating their back-office operations. Recently, there has been an emergence of online brokerages that offer a single multicurrency account for all three markets, futures, equities, and forex, with direct links to many exchanges worldwide. This bold step breaks the traditional fragmentation of brokerage services and everyone is now scrambling to implement the new technology to remain competitive. The globalization of brokerage services is in line with the globalization of every other economic activity in the world, and this provides more opportunity for profit but also risk of loss.

Trading is in principle a zero-sum game, and this will not change irrespective of any technological breakthrough. That is, the fact that in order for a trader to profit some other trader must lose in most cases will never change irrespective of any technological breakthrough in processing information on a global scale. Therefore, having a competitive advantage is much more important than any technological advance. Systematic trading combined with effective risk and money management can provide this much-needed competitive advantage in the new technological environment of fierce global competition.

CHAPTER 2

The Zero-Sum Game of Trading

Power and wisdom clash daily in the markets in a battle whose outcome determines how wealth is redistributed among market participants. At the end of each trading day, losses must equal profits. In other words, the sum of losses of all traders with losing positions, open or closed, must be equal to the sum of profits of traders with winning positions, minus commissions paid to brokerage houses, exchange fees, and any taxes paid to government.

The reader may have noticed that the losses were mentioned first and then equated to profits, instead of the other way around. These words were purposely so ordered that a skeptic could easily understand why trading is a zero-sum game—whether it is in equities, futures, or forex markets.

Losses are always the gains of the winners who take the opposite side of the trade. However, if one looks at the profits first, it is often difficult to understand why trading is a zero-sum-game, because part of the profits are not always due to trading. For example, profits may be realized from wealth-creating activities such as new technologies that open new markets and from dividend payments. In this respect, not all profits can be attributed to trading. However, all real losses from trading can be considered as profits made by other traders. Thus, trading is a zero-sum game by definition and cannot be considered otherwise because there is no wealth creation or destruction caused directly by the actions of market participants.

Moreover, trading does not create or destroy cash. Instead, the trading activity contributes only to a redistribution of wealth among participants. Investing any profits earned from trading in other sectors of the economy

17

might eventually generate wealth. Although there is a constant influx of new participants who join the trading game every day while others drop out, the zero-sum game nature of trading is not affected, simply because, as was already stated, this is the nature of trading by definition.

THE COUNTERARGUMENT

Some authors have challenged the notion that trading is a zero-sum game by arguing that it is not such since the bankroll is not fixed in advance. But such argument is naive. Even in a game of poker, where players may at any time borrow money and increase their bet size, the bankroll is not known in advance. What is known, though, with certainty is that one player will win what is lost by the rest. In a similar way, for every trading transaction that involves two traders, one of the traders will win and the other will lose if they both offset their position at the same time.

As such, it is very important that every market participant reach a clear understanding of what a zero-sum game involves and how it affects the chances of accumulating wealth from the trading activity. Simply said, the only way to make money by trading the markets is to have other traders lose. This is, at the highest level, accomplished by putting either power or wisdom, or both, to work and in such a way as to profit from the losses of other traders or investors. There is no cash machine printing money in the markets so that all participating traders can be winners. At the end of each trading day, the net loss must equal the net profit.

THE WINNERS AND LOSERS

Professional traders clearly understand market realities such as the zero-sum game. It is remarkable that many participants in the markets, especially small-account retail traders, do not realize that what they are essentially doing is aiming at the pockets of other participants. It is true that there are always some traders who are willing to lose because for them trading is a recreational activity, or it is a form of addiction whose financial outcome is of no importance so that they are doomed to lose. In Chapter 5, it will be shown that it is quite difficult to exercise effective risk and money management with a small account size and the probability of ruin is very high. This is the main reason why 95 percent of retail traders lose money.

The bulk of profits of the winners in a zero-sum game of trading do not come from the small account traders but from deep pockets, like overleveraged hedge funds that overestimate their capability to forecast price direction and underestimate the determination of other participants to grab their cash. Wall Street has a long history of speculative investment funds going belly up—no need to mention names here—because their managers made the wrong trading decisions, failed to exercise proper risk and money management, or overestimated their power or wisdom. It boils down to this: As soon as a new trading account is opened, whether a retail or corporate account, it becomes the potential target of millions of other traders. Anyone planning to participate in a zero-sum game and desires to profit from such activity must understand its mechanics and take all measures to assure that his or her funds are not redistributed to others. This translates directly into taking manageable risk while at the same time having a profitable systematic trading or investment strategy in place.

ZERO-SUM TRADING MARKETS

Commodity futures and forex trading are zero-sum games, by definition. For every buyer of a futures or currency contract there must be a seller and vice versa, because this is mandated by the operational structure of such markets.

Let us say, for example, that trader A purchases one futures contract of commodity XYZ, by posting $3,000 margin, from trader B, who sells the contract by also posting $3,000 margin. Trader A is said to have opened a long position and trader B a short position. Trader A expects prices to move up and trader B expects them to fall. Both traders expect to profit from their action, otherwise they would not have participated in the transaction. This is very trivial, but also important to understand. The two traders, A and B, have the exact opposite view about the direction of market prices in their specific time frame—intraday, short term, medium term, or even longer term. Both believe they are capable and smart individuals and can forecast price direction with a sufficiently high rate of success. If prices move straight up 3 points and both traders close their open positions at the same time, trader A makes 3 points and trader B loses 3 points. In reality, trader A makes less than 3 points and trader B loses more than 3 points, because of commissions paid to brokers and fees to exchanges. This is a simple case that illustrates the zero-sum game nature of trading.

It is possible that both A and B profit from the trade, but this cannot change the fact that the overall activity is a zero-sum game. Such a possibility often reinforces common illusions in thinking that trading is not a zero-sum game, but a misunderstanding of the mechanics involved is the real reason for them. Profits or losses can be evaluated at any time, even in real-time just after every price tick. In reality, any credit or debit posted to a trader's accounts occurs after the market closes and any open positions are marked-to-market using settlement prices. As an example, it is possible that before trader A closes his open long position, trader B closes his open short position by purchasing a contract offered by another seller, trader C, while prices are 2 points below the price level at which he and trader A opened their positions. In this case, trader B makes 2 points while trader A has an open position loss. If prices reverse to the upside after the decline, trader C may buy a contract sold by another trader, trader D, for a loss of 2 points to cover his short position. Then, trader D may buy a contract offered from trader A for a loss of 1 point. Now, trader A has a flat position. It is easy to calculate that although traders A and B made a total of 3 points, traders C and D lost 3 points and thus profits equal losses, as was expected. It does not matter how many traders participate and how many of them profit or lose. By definition, profits must equal losses and this simply means that the losses of some traders become the profits of some other traders.

In the case of forex trading and futures contracts, which are usually priced based on some underlying commodity, financial index, or security, it is fairly straightforward to see why trading is a zero-sum game. This is because for every buyer there must be a seller and the number of open long contracts always equals the number of open short contracts.

In the case of equity trading, things are a bit more complicated. One difference is that stock prices move due to either trading activity or wealth creation, or both. There is also short-selling activity allowed in certain securities, meaning the ability to borrow securities and sell them with the intention to buy them back later, return them to the borrower, and profit from the price difference.

Short sellers and stock lenders are engaged in a zero-sum game as in the case of futures contract trading. Losses are realized when a trader sells a security short by borrowing it, and although the expectation is that it will drop in price the opposite occurs and the trader is forced to purchase it back at a higher price in the future. The reverse holds if the security drops in price. In that case, the short-seller profits by covering the short position at a lower price.

RARE EXCEPTIONS TO THE RULE

Trading may not be a zero-sum game but a positive-sum game when there is underlying wealth creation. This is illustrated in the case of the stock of Microsoft Corporation (MSFT) and indicated as the "wealth creation

FIGURE 2.1 Wealth creation, bubble market, and bubble burst phases.
Source: APS Automatic Pattern Search.

period" in Figure 2.1. During the period 1996–1998, the price of the stock soared because the company was generating tremendous wealth by developing and introducing innovative new software technologies and rapidly expanding its market share worldwide.

Excluding any short-selling activity, during upward-trending markets powered mainly by wealth creation, investing, or even trading equities may be a positive-sum game. In reality, some traders realize losses even under such favorable conditions because price volatility forces them to take a loss, although the stock is in a strong uptrend. However, in markets where there is wealth creation, all traders can theoretically profit by sharing part of that wealth. But this is an exception to the rule and a rare opportunity. Periods of wealth creation are indeed rare; it is at the same time very difficult to identify using technical analysis alone whether there is actually wealth created or the upward-trending price is due to a bubble market.

Often, bubble markets follow wealth creation periods and exhibit a very steep rise in prices just before they burst. This is indicated in Figure 2.1 as the "bubble market period," which lasted for a whole year during 1999. The dramatic decline in prices that followed, shown as "bubble burst period," was dominated by zero-sum game trading. The losses of those who bought the stock during the bubble market rise became the profits of those who bought during the wealth creation period and held onto their positions. This is because early traders always satisfy the demand of late traders who scramble to get out when the bubble starts bursting. However, the primary beneficiaries of bubble markets are usually the major stockholders of a public company. They have a high incentive to sell to panicked traders and investors at high price levels and then repurchase their shares at a later time at a much lower price and thus maintain their percentage of ownership. If a stock is on an uptrend for reasons other than wealth creation, trading or investing is a zero-sum game. The losers are mostly individual traders and speculative funds and the winners are company insiders and longer-term investment funds.

DEALING WITH THE REALITIES OF THE ZERO-SUM GAME

Some have argued that a trader who is rational should never elect to participate in a zero-sum game where all participants have the same access to information and have the same skills, tools, and analysis capability. In such zero-sum games the longer-term expected profit is zero minus commissions. Instead, rational traders will look for markets where there is underlying wealth creation, like the equity markets, or a high number of unskilled participants, as in forex markets. The hope of underlying wealth creation appears to be the main reason why there are many more traders participating in equity markets than in futures or forex markets. However, I argue that choosing a market to trade based solely on the criterion of wealth creation is—due to a wrong assessment of the situation—a wrong decision. Wherever there is wealth creation there are also those who control it or have access to it and will eventually use it to their advantage and benefit. For instance, those who control wealth creation can affect the rate of its creation by delaying business plans and thus causing a temporary halt or decline in equity prices in order to shake out weak hands. Also, company insiders can use their wealth to buy securities on margin and affect the slope of the price rise and its momentum. It seems, on the contrary, that a rational trader should better try outsmarting other rational traders, especially novice ones, in futures or forex markets, rather than trying to compete with company insiders, or even exchange specialists, in the equity markets. Insiders can sell shares at any time (provided they comply with regulations) and for any legal reason—for instance, for the purpose of buying a home, a yacht, or a diamond ring. There is no way of predicting such activity or motives, especially in companies with a small float—that is, with a good fraction of outstanding shares in the hands of the owners.

Why should anyone then be willing to trade equities unless there is wealth being created? Companies know that prospects of growth, a possible takeover, or mergers and so forth motivate traders and investors to participate in equity markets. In order to attract the buyers they need to absorb the supply created by insider selling and prevent prices from collapsing, they often issue favorable news releases just before the sale is to take place. Traders and investors just don't realize that when a good story about a company hits the wire and prices rally, someone is always selling to satisfy the created demand and that someone is hardly an irrational trader—most often an insider or a specialist. Therefore, from this particular perspective, participating as a trader in equity markets has many more disadvantages than in a pure zero-sum game like futures or forex markets.

The accumulated profits of rational and skilled traders in zero-sum game markets depend on a constant influx of unskilled and recreational traders who are destined to lose, and whose losses become the profits of the winners. Few of the unskilled traders will eventually survive the zero-sum game and turn profitable at the expense of other traders. Professional and commercial traders always have an advantage over individual retail traders, while a small fraction of technical traders—about 5 percent of them—are consistently making a profit. The zero-sum trading game is a very hard one to play, especially when there are players with better access to order flow, like specialists, market makers, or brokers trading for their own account. The only chances an individual trader or manager of a small fund who base trading decisions on the analysis of price and volume have depend on how innovative and disciplined they are in determining the timing of entry and exit points and managing risk. Profitability combined with risk and money management is the key to beating the odds of the zero-sum game.

This key to success also goes by the name *systematic trading* and requires, among other things, taking a quantitative approach to analyzing and understanding the concepts of profitability and risk; these are the subjects of Part II of the book, which includes Chapters 4 and 5. Only then one can move ahead and develop a winning trading methodology according to the principles described in the final part of this book.

CHAPTER 3

Trading Methods
and Time Frames

his chapter discusses the two methods that the majority of traders employ in analyzing and forecasting price direction: fundamental and technical analysis. These two popular trading methods are analyzed from the perspective of a market as defined in Chapter 1. This chapter also discusses trading time frames, intraday trading, short-term trading, and longer-term trading. Finally, some popular trading methods are presented through a combination of trading time frames.

Although these subjects are already covered extensively in the trading literature, the analysis in this chapter provides some interesting insight into the capabilities and limitations of the popular trading methods and concentrates on the advantages and disadvantages of the different trading time frames.

TRADING METHODS

There are two methods the majority of traders employ in the analysis of markets and in forecasting price direction: *Fundamental analysis (FA)* is based on macroeconomic and microeconomic factors and indicators derived from them. *Technical analysis (TA)* is based on chart studies and indicators using historical price and volume series. There are some other methods used by traders that are based on esoteric concepts, for instance, the use of astrology charts or analysis based on media effects or on crowd behavioral patterns, but these are beyond the scope of this book.

Proponents of FA argue that historical market prices alone cannot be used in forecasting price moves with a high probability of success and thus TA is an ineffective method. Proponents of TA respond that market prices, current and historical, fully reflect all factors that determine current price levels and thus FA is unnecessary. Each side argues against the effectiveness of the other but arguments about the effectiveness of its own method remain sketchy.

Users of both TA and FA have always tried to defend their method against the *efficient market hypothesis*, which considers the flow of information to be random and hence argues that prices move randomly. According to this famous hypothesis, if prices move randomly, then any effort to forecast their future direction is an exercise in futility. Despite these academic arguments and the heated debates that take place quite often in conferences or online forums dedicated to the subject, traders have many reasons to believe that price moves are not random for extended periods of time. Consequently, they concentrate on developing trading systems using either FA or TA.

In the next section, the two methods of analysis and forecasting of market prices are discussed from the perspective of a market as defined in Chapter 1 and illustrated in Figure 1.1.

Fundamental Analysis

A trader who employs fundamental analysis to develop trading systems is a participant of the market, as indicated by the small black square in Figure 3.1. Information about macroeconomic and microeconomic factors that drive the market is analyzed in the box labeled *FA* and the output is the forecast based on which the trader plans his or her actions.

Essentially, FA attempts to identify a mathematical model that can forecast price direction based on trends in fundamental parameters, which are part of the input information. This method assumes that there is a certain functional, or *causal*, relationship between information and prices that can be estimated by suitable quantitative models. However, if

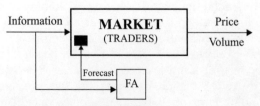

FIGURE 3.1 Fundamental analysis method.

during certain time periods the actions of the majority of market participants are driven by inputs other than fundamental information, for example, fear or greed, FA turns ineffective or even worthless. But if one makes the assumption that over the longer-term fundamentals and prices reach the state of a stable functional relationship, then FA can be effective in that longer time frame.

It appears then that the effectiveness of FA increases as a function of the trading time frame considered. Favorable news often results in intraday and short-term profit taking, and that is the reason "buy the rumor, sell the fact" seems to be true. Thus, the effectiveness of FA in intraday trading is limited by the participant's dynamic anticipatory behavior and that is extremely hard to model. The effectiveness of FA increases slightly in short-term trading, but it is not clear whether it can lead to high-profitability systematic trading methods. Higher effectiveness can be achieved in longer-term trading time frames and it appears that this is the appropriate domain for the application of FA.

However, critics argue that FA is not a quantitative method and thus it cannot be as systematic as TA. Perhaps that was true when fundamental information was both difficult to collect and expensive, something that only privileged market players could afford. Nowadays, there are software programs available for a low monthly fee with databases of fundamental parameters that update online and can be used in FA models to make quantitative predictions. Proper application of FA presupposes that traders have an excellent understanding of finance, economics, and mathematics so that they can develop such models. Therefore, FA is a task not suitable to the average trader, who would resort exclusively to TA instead and shorter trading time frames.

Technical Analysis

Traders using technical analysis to time price moves and act accordingly are participants of the market, as indicated by the small black square in Figure 3.2.

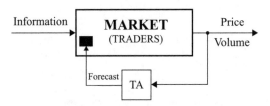

FIGURE 3.2 Technical analysis method.

Price and volume, current and historical, are used to develop trading systems that attempt to determine the timing of market entry and exit points with high enough probability of success so as to result in high profitability. There are a variety of technical analysis methods. Some are based on charting historical prices and identifying patterns, such as support/resistance levels, price retracement levels, or candlestick formations. Other methods are based on devising mathematical indicators and formulas that are in turn used to develop trading systems. TA methods can be implemented in programming languages and can be fully automated. This does not mean, however, that through the process of automation the full capability and effectiveness of those methods is realized, as this ultimately depends mainly on the risk and money management methods incorporated.

Nowadays, there are software programs that can be used to implement TA methods using high-level programming languages specifically designed for that task. These programs have a database of historical prices that regularly updates (even in real-time) so that the developed TA models can generate trading signals in the relevant time frames. Recent developments in this area include integration of such software programs with online order entry and direct execution platforms. This level of integration presents a complete solution to system development based on TA (or even FA) that incorporates automatic order placement and direct execution, as well as portfolio updating in real time. This sounds great as far as an application of software technology, but the key question is, how effective is it in reality in increasing profitability?

As may be seen in Figure 3.2, TA is a *closed-loop* approach in the sense that the output of the market is used as an input to the TA methodology and then fed back to the trader. But it is not quite a closed-loop system in the sense that the forecast does not become part of the input to the whole market but just to a single trader, or group of traders, who otherwise ignore the market input information. However, if many traders use the same TA models, their output can be assumed to be part of the information that drives the actions of a good portion of the market participants.

If a large number of participants use TA to affect trading decisions, then the actions of those participants do not depend on fundamental information that usually drives the markets, but rather on TA. Then, under these conditions, TA output becomes a self-fulfilling prophecy. When the actions of the majority of market participants are *not* based on fundamentals but are essentially driven by TA, prices can become very volatile. Prices and volatility return to equilibrium levels dictated by fundamental valuations when participants who base decisions on fundamental factors start dominating.

As evidenced by the discussion above, TA can be effective in all time frames but the profitability of systematic trading methods based on it

depends on several factors external to the method, such as human inter-
ference in executing trades and periods of ineffective operation due to
low liquidity. TA methods must be combined with effective risk and money
management to limit losses during the periods that such methods become
ineffective.

Combining Technical and Fundamental Analysis

FA and TA can be combined to form a hybrid trading methodology. There
are software programs in the marketplace that provide such capability. Hybrid methodologies are more effective in longer-term trading and of great
value to long-term investors and investment managers. Combining technical and fundamental analysis allows value investing combined with an
identification of technical price levels for active portfolio management.
For example:

- Investors and fund managers can use FA to screen a universe of securities and identify stocks with good fundamentals and earnings growth
  potential. Then, they can use TA to determine the timing to purchase
  shares, such as near oversold levels or after a retracement of prices of
  a certain percentage from the peak of a rally.
- Company treasurers can use FA to forecast the longer-term trend of
  currency prices and thus the earnings from their international operations in base currency, while TA can assist in deciding when to hedge
  transactions or take a calculated risk.
- Interest rate and index futures traders can use FA to establish longer-
  term trends and TA to determine the timing of market entry and exit.
- Index-tracking funds can use FA models to establish longer-term
  trends of equity prices and interest rates and TA models in an effort
  to outperform benchmark index returns.

TRADING TIME FRAMES

One of the most common classifications of traders is made according
to the trading time frame in which they operate. The three trading time
frames that traders operate in are *intraday, short-term,* or *longer-term*
time frames. Of course, nothing prevents a trader from operating in all
three trading time frames. As a matter of fact, many trade in all three basic time frames depending on market conditions among other things. It
is understood by such market participants that each different time frame

demands different skills and, more importantly, different trading methodologies and hardware/software setups.

In this section I describe each trading time frame from the perspective of these basic differences and then offer an example of how time frames can be combined in a trading methodology.

Intraday Trading

Intraday traders attempt to profit from small price excursions during trading sessions. Open positions have an average duration of a few seconds to a few hours, depending on the model used and also on how fast the trader's platform can route orders to the exchange and execute them. With the advent of screen trading, online order placement, and direct execution, buyers and sellers are matched in an efficient manner using sophisticated order book handling algorithms and at the same time orders are executed in split-seconds. The increasing demand for efficient intraday executions has given rise to the development of *ATSs* (alternative trading systems) based on *algorithmic trading* techniques and the emergence of *dark liquidity pools* that operate independently of the main exchanges and match buyers to sellers. There is more to come in this area, as there is growing demand for more efficient executions and for attracting liquidity in order for brokers to stay competitive. Intraday traders can take advantage of all these new developments to increase their profitability.

Profiting from intraday price moves and volatility requires timely access to the information provided by the various exchanges, *ECNs* (electronic communication networks), and other liquidity pools. Technical intraday traders can monitor price, volume, and market depth in real time and use trading systems to generate entry and exit signals and to automatically place orders. By the end of the trading day, intraday traders are "flat" and thus do not carry any open positions overnight. This is an advantage over short-term or longer-term trading, but the main gain is probably psychological.

There is no evidence that intraday trading can be more profitable than trading based on the other time frames. On the contrary, some have questioned the longer-term profitability of intraday trading. The main disadvantage of intraday trading is that during slow or illiquid markets some participants of markets that operate based on open outcry, also known as *locals*, can "run" the stops of intraday traders. The same can happen in markets based on screen trading, where market makers or other big players dominate. However, any intraday market fluctuations caused by such activity do not affect the short-term trend of prices.

The issue of commissions is another reason why critics question whether intraday trading is more profitable than trading based on other time frames. Commissions paid to brokers impact the profitability of intraday traders. Many intraday traders end up working very hard for their brokers, who profit from the commissions they get, while the traders assume all the risk. Commissions accumulate fast in intraday trading and at the end of the year can sum up to a good percentage of any profits made or may even exceed them. Therefore, one of the primary tasks of intraday traders is finding the lowest commission rate available for their market.

The ultimate beneficiaries of the intraday zero-sum trading game are the brokerages that earn commissions with relatively low or no risk. The longer-term effect of commissions paid is a reduction of total trading capital and thus the diminishing financial power of traders. The effect of commissions on profitability will be approached in Chapter 4 from a quantitative perspective. Qualitatively, just a small fraction of retail traders who trade intraday will end up accumulating wealth through such activity.

Intraday trading poses two important questions:

1. Can retail traders with a small or moderate account size eventually profit from intraday trading?
2. What are the necessary skills for achieving profitability in intraday trading?

There are no easy answers in theory, but experience provides some general guidelines. The remainder of this section on intraday trading will deal primarily with some answers to these questions.

The majority of intraday retail traders cannot stay profitable over extended periods of time because they do not have a competitive advantage over market makers and other professionals who understand the mechanics of markets and have better access to order flow and information. It is true that the advent of screen trading and the availability of order book depth information has closed the gap significantly between professionals and retail traders. But access to information cannot make up for high purchasing power, control of liquidity, and the ability to move prices in a preferred direction.

It is also true that the particular style of intraday trading adopted can impact profitability. Intraday traders may be classified according to the method they use and their objectives. Most small-account retail traders with virtually no power to influence price direction attempt to forecast intraday price changes using real-time charting software and technical analysis. Others just use their experience in "reading the tape." Some traders with sufficiently large accounts attempt to scalp the order book using available depth information and profit from the bid–ask spreads.

In the equity markets, scalpers take advantage of low commission rates but need to trade bigger size in order to profit. If they are caught with an open position while an unpredictable and sudden intraday change in prices happens against them, they can lose many months' accumulated profits in a single trade. Since the direction of prices of most liquid stocks is positively correlated with that of major stock indexes, any sudden intraday fluctuations in stock prices may be caused by economic or political developments rather than being the result of technical trading activity. Thus, trading large size for the purpose of profiting from bid–ask spreads or minute price excursions or attempting to scalp the order book carries a high risk due to random factors influencing price direction. As a result, most intraday traders who get involved in such activity eventually face these disturbing market realities and quit trading after losing substantial sums of money.

Regarding the profitability of intraday trading, it has been argued by many that TA methods cannot effectively forecast intraday price direction with a high rate of success. This is because intraday price changes are mostly random and are caused by the collective actions of market participants who have different objectives and motivations. Only under special and rare circumstances is intraday price direction predictable. This happens when the actions of market participants are influenced by certain factors that dominate over all other factors that can affect trading decisions and cause prices to move in specific directions. Examples of such factors are unexpected economic news and other events having to do with significant political developments on a regional or global scale.

However, it is important to realize that the success rate of technical methods during periods dominated by random or unexpected events carries low statistical significance. It does not reflect an inherent capability of such methods to forecast price direction; the effect is due only to the underlying momentum of market prices without any regard to its cause.

Next, before turning our attention to the question regarding the required skills and tools, we must note that the number of individuals who trade intraday has increased dramatically over the last three decades. The increase has been almost geometric, conforming, in principle, to the increase in the growth of information technology. This phenomenal increase in the number of intraday traders has been accompanied by an increase in the number of online brokerages. Such brokerages offer real-time order placement and direct executions, technical analysis applications, and fundamental economic data, as well as news and research about every available market sector and traded instrument. With such advanced tools available at low cost or even free with the opening of an account, intraday trading sounds like a perfect setup for those dreaming of becoming independently wealthy while working from the comfort of their home. But this is not the reality of the situation.

Intraday trading is probably one of the most demanding jobs one could do for a living and imposes serious mental and physical fatigue on a trader. It is a job best suited for young and energetic people just out of college and operating in a structured environment, like the dealing room of an investment firm, and under strict supervision in terms of the risk they can assume and methodology followed, as set by senior management. This is not a job for someone who is looking for comfort and lower stress.

Intraday trading is also a *two-shift* job. During the first shift, the market trading hours, there is heavy activity demanding high concentration; during the second shift, the trader must research new methods, develop systems, and analyze performance. Both shifts are demanding, but there is especially great physical and mental stress during the first shift. Of course, there are always exceptions, those who are gifted with unique abilities, strength, and endurance, but they are just that, exceptions to the rule.

There are numerous factors, some already discussed, that can adversely affect the already-low chances of becoming wealthy by trading intraday that a person with average capabilities cannot deal with effectively. Of course, this does not mean that one should not try to beat the intraday zero-sum game odds. When market realities are understood and profit expectations are kept at reasonable levels, the chances of winning are greatly improved.

Short-Term Trading

Although one can find several definitions of short-term trading, in principle this type of trading time frame involves open positions that last more than a day. Short-term traders are essentially position traders, meaning that they attempt to profit by holding open positions overnight. Open positions can be held for several days or even weeks depending on what notion of *short-term* one adopts. Some short-term traders open positions without any regard to the direction of the medium or longer-term trend; others pay close attention to price direction and momentum.

Short-term trading has certain advantages, but also disadvantages when compared with intraday trading. The major advantage of short-term trading over intraday trading is that profit target and stop-loss levels can be set sufficiently away from the entry price and thus are not subjected to intraday price swings. Thus, a short-term trader does not have to worry about volatility caused by intraday traders, unless prices move close to her stops. If the short-term price direction forecast is correct, then the position will generate a profit regardless of intraday volatility and market swings.

Wide equity swings caused by large drawdowns can be a major disadvantage of short-term trading. To remedy the situation, a short-term trader must adjust position size accordingly. Reducing position size in proportion to trading capital results in reduced exposure and a lower impact of price swings and gaps in equity performance. However, it also results in a reduction in realized profit. The right balance between position size and risk ultimately determines the longer-term equity performance of short-term trading, but it also imposes additional constraints on trading system design and account capitalization, as will be further discussed in Chapters 4 and 5.

The primary cause of losses in short-term trading time frames is due to the wrong timing of market entry and exit signals. Opening a position a day in advance or a day later can make the difference between realizing a profit or a loss. As in the case of intraday prices, short-term prices move most of the time in a random fashion. The difficult task of a short-term trader involves the identification of periods during which randomness gives way to a degree of certainty. This is an exceptionally difficult forecasting problem, because market conditions and therefore the actions of market participants are constantly changing. But that is not the only difficulty present in short-term trading system design.

The most important factor that affects the performance of short-term traders, besides the profitability of the trading system used, is the psychological burden imposed by leaving positions open overnight, especially when the positions are losing money. But it is not only unrealized losses that can affect the psychology of a short-term trader; it is also the unrealized profits. When an open position is profitable, short-term traders are often tempted to close it and realize the profit, even if the profit target set in advance has not be reached. Such emotive actions can lead to compulsive trading decisions and adversely affect the profitability of a system because of their direct effect on the average-win-to-average-loss ratio. Profitability and the ratio of average win to average loss are related in a unique way, as will be shown in Chapter 4, where the *profitability rule* is derived. Most short-term traders tend to overshoot their preset loss levels and undershoot profit targets—something that adversely impacts the expected ratio of average win to average loss and in turn results in lower profitability.

In order to limit the effects of compulsive actions, short-term traders often place *GTC* (good till canceled) stop-loss orders and profit target limit orders at the same time, as a *bracket order*, after a position is opened. These types of orders can provide some psychological comfort and are highly recommended for the reasons just discussed, provided of course that the liquidity of the traded markets can effectively accommodate such orders without a negative impact on profitability.

Short-term traders use a variety of technical analysis approaches for the purpose of devising a profitable method of entering and exiting the market. The majority of technical analysis indicators and formulas, such as moving averages, *MACD* (moving average convergence/divergence), and

DMI (directional moving index), to mention just a few, are not very effective in timing short-term price direction with an accuracy required for sufficiently high profitability. Such indicators exhibit a lag in following prices that is undesirable when dealing with short-term price fluctuations. The lag is due to the averaging or summation of prices, an operation that smoothes volatility. More importantly, use of indicators for opening and exiting positions often results in optimized systems, because there are variables involved and their values can be set for optimum historical performance. Timing lag and optimization form an explosive cocktail, but most beginner short-term traders understand that only after a substantial loss is realized.

Analysis of chart formations is very popular among short-term traders. Traditional chart pattern formations such as triangles, heads-and-shoulders, and double bottoms first must be confirmed, and this also results in a significant time lag, often much larger than that of indicators. In addition, the timing of exits requires some other method to be used. The end result is that short-term trading system development based on indicators and chart patterns is fraught with difficulties. Price patterns have proven much more effective in dealing with timing and optimization issues. Price patterns are chart formations, similar to traditional chart patterns, that can be used with a profit target and stop-loss to develop trading systems for short-term trading. Price patterns cannot be optimized as far as generating the entry signals. However, robust price patterns are difficult to identify visually and a systematic process must be employed for that purpose. Some examples of a systematic approach to price pattern identification and trading system development are provided in Chapter 7 and code is included in the appendix.

Commissions charged in short-term trading do not have as detrimental an effect on equity performance as on intraday trading. Furthermore, some short-term trading methods do not require monitoring prices intraday, and any stop-loss and profit target orders can be placed when a position is opened. This allows more time for trading system development or even activities not related to trading.

Longer-Term Trading

The objective of a longer-term trader is to follow a trend for as long as there is a profit to be made. This type of trading is also called *trend trading* or *trend following*. The trend duration may be several months or even years, depending on objectives. Longer-term traders use a variety of fundamental and technical methods in order to determine possible points of trend initiation and reversal, or trend entry and exit. Capturing a trend in prices and successfully following it is probably the dream of every serious trader or investor.

Longer-term trading has the highest profit potential when compared with intraday and short-term trading because the trader can slowly accumulate positions along the direction of the trend. Many longer-term traders do not perceive their activity to be a full-time job and have other occupations—a luxury an intraday trader does not have and a short-term trader may or may not have depending on the particular methodology employed.

Then, why do most traders prefer intraday or short-term trading? As will be discussed at length in the following, trends are hard to identify and follow. In addition, it is even harder to determine when a trend reversal is pending and it is time to close open positions. Furthermore, it is quite hard to execute profitable systematic trading methodologies for trend following due to the emotional burden caused by holding open positions for an extended period of time Thus, there are several reasons why traders decide not to attempt to follow price trends. The three most important are:

1. Trends can be defined with certainty only in hindsight.
2. There are no robust trend-trading indicators or systems.
3. The psychological burden on a longer-term trader is too high.

A trend in prices can be identified with certainty only after a significant portion of it has already been formed. People refer to the tendency to assign high probability, or even certainty, to events after they happen as *hindsight*. More importantly, every price level along a trend can become the starting point of a reversal, so there is no guarantee that an already-identified trend will stay in place. There are no technical analysis methods that can determine with high certainty whether prices will continue rising or falling so that a trend will be sustained. This is because a trend can be established only by analyzing historical market prices.

Buyers match sellers exactly at all price levels on a trend and the only factor that affects direction is *price concession*. When buyers concede to higher sell offers, prices trend up, and the opposite happens when sellers concede to lower buy offers, but that can change at any time due to market participants changing their short-term outlook about fundamental valuations. Trends develop in all markets and their presence, although it can be established with certainty only in hindsight, is an empirical fact. But experience about any particular market conditions refers only to the past, which is an irreversible process. Time direction cannot be reversed and experience can be useful only as far as making decisions regarding future market conditions.

Besides being very difficult to identify, trends are also time-subjective. Figure 3.3 shows a weekly chart of Dow Jones Industrials from 1988 to

FIGURE 3.3 Trendlines depend on the time horizon.
Source: Metastock charts courtesy of Equis International, a Reuters company.

mid-2003. Two trendlines are drawn on the chart and indicated as *T1* and *T2*. Trendline T1 indicates a trend in prices that started in 1988. Trendline T2 indicates a different trend, with a steeper slope, that started in late 1994 and ended in mid-2001, when the prices crossed the line to the downside. Letters *A* through *G* shown on the chart are used in the following in reference to price action taking place at the time period they correspond to.

From the presence of the two trendlines, T1 and T2, on the same weekly chart, it is evident that any reference to a *trend* must be accompanied by another reference to a *relevant time horizon*. Unfortunately, this leads to excessive subjectivity. A longer-term trader who follows trendline T1 would assert that the index is still on an uptrend as of the last day on the chart, as shown in Figure 3.3, regardless of the increase in volatility after year 1999 and the subsequent decline in prices. Another trader, who follows trendline T2, could argue that prices have ended their uptrend and are now in a downtrend. The interesting part of this example is that both views are consistent within the technical analysis framework; at the same time they are valid only in hindsight.

Note that from price action alone one could not determine with certainty at the time of their occurrence whether points A through D could mark the end of the trend, and any decisions to stay invested should be based on other factors, such as fundamental analysis. The same holds true in the case of the decline that followed the peak in prices at point E. Technical analysis of price and volume alone could not provide any certainty that a trend reversal to the upside at points F or G could not have occurred. Only fundamental factors can provide some indication about the longer-term direction of prices.

Technical traders who understand how sudden price corrections in trending markets can affect the performance of technical indicators, especially those used to develop trend-following systems, know that the effectiveness of such methods is very limited. Sudden trend reversals can result in devastating reductions of unrealized open position profits or can turn a profitable trade into a loss. Such events usually have a negative impact on the psychology of a longer-term trader besides affecting profitability. Even experienced traders feel the emotional burden caused by holding open positions for extended periods of time and thus being subject to the possibility of adverse gap openings or sudden trend reversals. It is only natural, then, that many longer-term traders are constantly tempted to pull the trigger and pocket profits after a favorable short-term price rally. But patience is a virtue in longer-term trading, and the proper psychology plays as important a role as any good trading methodology and analysis.

Whoever can effectively deal with these problems, even partially, has a ticket to becoming extremely wealthy.

Trading in Multiple Time Frames

Some popular trading methods are based on a combination of trading time frames. These methods usually specify a primary trading time frame based on which market entry points are determined and use other trading time frames to identify the exit points, as well as to manage open position size and risk. The two trading methods that we will examine are *intraday/short-term trading* and *short-term/longer-term trading*.

Intraday/Short-Term Trading   In this popular trading time frame combination, intraday price bars are used to establish market entry and exit points. When the intraday time frame is used as primary, entry signals may be determined on any intraday bar period, such as 30-minute or hourly bars. There are two steps involved:

1. Longer time periods are used to establish the short-term trend and thus whether to open a long or a short position.
2. Shorter time periods are used for position management and position exiting.

Step 1 is also used to filter out entry signals that go against the trend and can be subject to an immediate reversal or correction in prices. Step 2

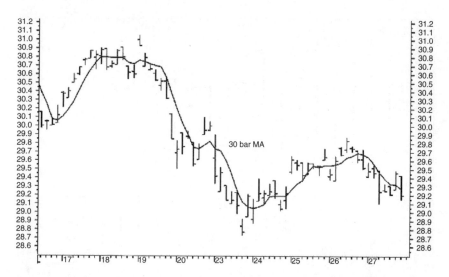

FIGURE 3.4 Using a moving average of hourly bars to establish the short-term trend.
Source: Metastock charts courtesy of Equis International, a Reuters company.

is used in addition to increase profitability by taking advantage of intra-day price volatility. This is usually achieved by selling peaks and buy-ing the bottoms of intraday price reversals. Step 2 is much more diffi-cult to implement because it requires a model for timing intraday price reversals.

This method is illustrated in Figure 3.4, which shows an hourly bar chart of the stock of Intel Corp. with a simple moving average plotted on it. The moving average slope is used as an indication of the short-term trend. Long positions are established based on a signal by an inside day pattern formed on the daily chart shown in Figure 3.5. Half of the long position is sold when prices reach for a second time the upper trendline of a rising channel of 15-minute bars, as shown in Figure 3.6. When the lower trend-line of the channel is violated to the downside, the remaining half position is sold. In this method of combining time frames, position entry is estab-lished based on daily and intraday prices and position exiting is determined based on intraday prices. The main advantage in combining trading time frames this way is the possibility of a higher average selling price.

Short-Term/Longer-Term Trading   In this combination of trading time frames, short-term trading based on daily price bars is used to ef-fectively achieve trend following. The basic idea behind this method is to break longer-term trends into shorter-term trends that can be identified

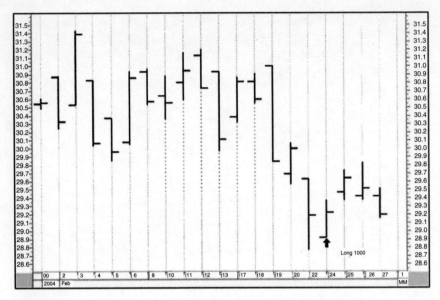

FIGURE 3.5 Inside day pattern in daily data used as entry signals.
Source: Metastock charts courtesy of Equis International, a Reuters company.

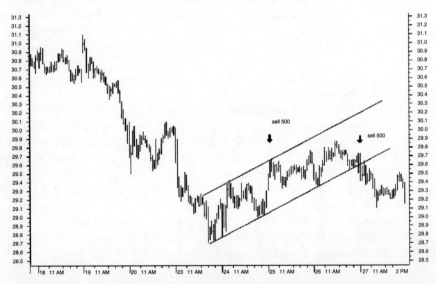

FIGURE 3.6 Rising channel in 15-minute bars used to determine exit points.
Source: Metastock charts courtesy of Equis International, a Reuters company.

based on technical methods and thus avoid having to develop a trend-following trading system. This method requires a short-term trading strategy that can generate enough signals along the direction of a trend to capture a significant portion of a move in prices. Therefore, the longer-term performance from following the trend comes as an added benefit of a systematic short-term trading methodology. The entry-signal generation of such systems can be based on a multitude of criteria and cover a wide range of conditions that may occur along the trend. For example, a simple 5–30 daily bar moving average crossover can be used for that purpose, as shown in Figure 3.7.

A simple trend-following method based on elementary smoothing indicators, such as moving averages, can be very effective in determining entry points, but establishing the exit point is very hard. For instance, after opening a long position at the simple moving average crossover point B shown in Figure 3.7, the intraday price reversals at points E1 and E2 can force closing the position with a small profit. It is quite hard, given the volatility in prices, to keep the open position and exit at point E, where the moving average crossover occurs to the downside, and thus capture a good portion of the trend.

For the majority of traders who do not have the experience and psychology to follow trends, the philosophy of an alternative method is illustrated in Figure 3.8. The price trend of Figure 3.7 is now broken down

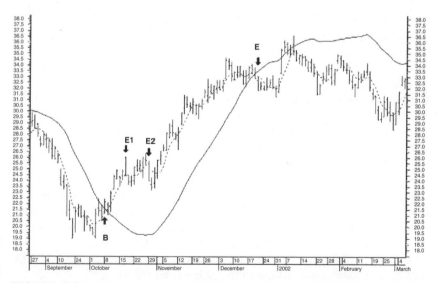

FIGURE 3.7 Using a simple moving average crossover as the entry signal.
Source: Metastock charts courtesy of Equis International, a Reuters company.

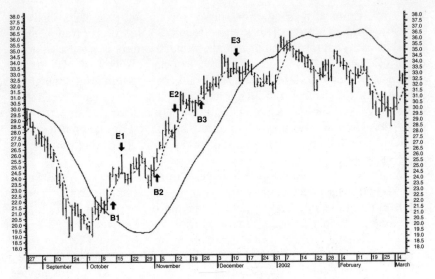

FIGURE 3.8 Breaking up a trend into three shorter-term trends.
Source: Metastock charts courtesy of Equis International, a Reuters company.

into three intermediate shorter-term trends using high-profitability price patterns to generate entry and exit signals. The technique is based on a short-term trading time frame, but the added benefit is that it can be repeated over a longer-term time frame. The three consecutive market entry points labeled *B1*, *B2*, and *B3* are exited at the corresponding points *E1*, *E2*, and *E3* using a predetermined profit target. A trend-following technique is not used in this method, but the approach can theoretically match or even exceed the performance of classical longer-term trading methods. However, designing trading systems based on short-term trading time frames to capture trends is not a trivial task; more on this subject will be mentioned in Chapter 7, where trading system synthesis is discussed.

When the two methods of analysis and forecasting price direction, namely fundamental and technical analysis, are viewed from the perspective of the market defined in Chapters 1, as was done in this chapter, then advantages and limitations become clearer. If such analysis is combined with a realistic account of the different trading time frames, as was done, a better understanding of the trading game can be developed. When such understanding is further combined with quantitative approaches to profitability and risk and money management, which are the subjects of Chapters 4 and 5, then the foundations are set for developing systematic trading methodologies that are both realistic and potentially profitable.

PART II

Profitability and Risk

Systematic trading methodologies offer great potential for consistent and robust performance if all the parameters that affect profitability are well understood and rigorously quantified. An equation that involves some of these parameters, the *profitability rule*, is discussed in Chapter 4. This equation provides, among other things, valuable insight into some of the constraints imposed on profitability by the realities of markets and trading system operation.

Risk and money management must be an integral part of every successful trading methodology. In Chapter 5, the *fundamental law of risk and money management* is presented. This is a simple rule every trader should understand and apply constantly; however, in reality many pay little attention to its straightforward results. Any advanced risk and money management techniques used in trading system development can be successful provided that the basic requirements set by this simple law are met and it is effectively used to calculate risk and position size.

An understanding of the meaning and implications of the profitability rule and the fundamental law of risk and money management is essential for the success of systematic trading methodologies.

CHAPTER 4

The Profitability Rule

T he profitability rule is a simple yet extremely important equation that relates the profitability of a trading system—also referred to as the *success rate*—to its profit factor and average winning to average losing trade. In this chapter, I present a derivation of the profitability rule and then discuss some of the tradeoffs and limitations it imposes on trading system design and performance. I also discuss the impact of the profitability rule on the various trading time frames and derive a more general equation that takes into account commissions and slippage.

QUALITATIVE VERSUS QUANTITATIVE

Those who decide to adopt a systematic approach to trading end up allocating significant time and resources toward the development of mechanical systems. When developing such systems, one can easily get lost in a maze of technical analysis indicators that are known to perform poorly, not only based on historical testing but also in actual trading. The poor performance of most technical trading systems, often developed using platforms available to retail traders, is mainly due to the limited ability of most technical analysis methods to time price direction in an accurate and consistent manner.

Another factor contributing to poor performance is the lack of an understanding of the fundamental tradeoffs imposed on trading system design by the relation of profitability, profit factor, and ratio of average winning to average losing trade. The result of this lack of understanding of the basic relationships that govern the behavior of trading systems is the imposition of unnecessary constraints during the development process.

There are several references in the trading literature to the fact that the ratio of average winning to average losing trade, the profit factor, and the profitability of a trading system are related quantitatively. One can find such references in articles and books dealing mainly with position sizing, because some of the formulas presented there involve some of the abovementioned parameters. An example is the well-known *Kelly formula*.

At the same time, one might have difficulty finding an explanation as to why these parameters are related and how to derive an equation that can be used by trading system developers. Even worse, qualitative references to such a mathematical relationship lacking any quantitative content seem more to generate confusion than to illuminate the problems inherent in trading system development. Statements like "It's good to have an average win/loss ratio of 2:1 or greater," or "Let your profits run and cut your losses short," provide no explanation about the underlying deduction process used to arrive at them.

Furthermore, vague guidelines of this sort may impose unnecessary limitations on the development of trading methodologies and often turn out to be false or bad advice. It is known that the literature in the trading system development field, other than a few exceptions, is plagued with vague and unjustifiable statements that are not backed by any mathematical derivation. However, readers should know that any proposed rule that is not backed by a quantitative derivation is potentially false and advice based on it is ultimately damaging or, at best, unnecessarily limiting. This will become evident from the discussion on the derivation of the profitability rule.

DERIVATION OF THE PROFITABILITY RULE

A trading system is profitable over a period of time T, if the amount of winning trades is greater than the amount of losing trades over that period. If we denote the amount of winning trades by the sum of winning trades and the amount of losing trades by the sum of losing trades, the following must hold for all profitable systems:

$$\sum_T W - \sum_T L > 0 \qquad (4.1)$$

The average winning trade is defined as the sum of winning trades divided by their number:

$$\overline{W} = \frac{\sum_T W}{N_W} \qquad (4.2)$$

where N_W is the number of winning trades. Similarly, the average losing trade is defined as:

$$\overline{L} = \frac{\sum_T L}{N_L} \qquad (4.3)$$

where N_L is the number of losing trades. By combining equations 4.1, 4.2, and 4.3, we obtain

$$\overline{W}N_W - \overline{L}N_L > 0 \qquad (4.4)$$

The number of winning plus the number of losing trades equals the total number of trades N, by definition. Therefore:

$$N_L = N - N_W \qquad (4.5)$$

By combining equations 4.4 and 4.5 and after dividing through by $N > 0$ we obtain:

$$\overline{W}\frac{N_W}{N} - \overline{L}\frac{N - N_W}{N} > 0 \qquad (4.6)$$

Next, we define the profitability P, also referred to as the success rate, as the ratio of the number of wining trades N_W to the total number of trades N. As a result, P is a fraction that ranges from 0 to 1 (or from 0 to 100% when expressed as a percentage):

$$P = \frac{N_W}{N} \qquad (4.7)$$

After introducing equation 4.7 into equation 4.6, we obtain:

$$\overline{W}P - \overline{L}(1 - P) > 0 \qquad (4.8)$$

If the profitability P is assumed to be equal to the probability of win, then equation 4.8 tells us that the expected gain of a profitable system when a signal is generated is always greater than zero. Specifically, the probability of win times the average win minus the probability of loss times the average loss is the expected gain E(g) of a trading system:

$$E(g) = \overline{W}P - \overline{L}(1 - P) \tag{4.9}$$

The expected gain E(g) of a profitable trading system is always greater than zero. It is easy to see from equation 4.9 that when tossing a fair coin, in which case P = 0.5, with an average win equal to the average loss, the expected gain E(g) is zero. For a positive expected gain, it is the relation of profitability to the ratio of average win to average loss that matters, not their specific values. As a matter of fact, high profitability does not suffice to have a winning trading system, as is evident from equation 4.9. Thus, we can proceed to derive a more general expression that reveals the unique relationship of the parameters involved.

The average losing trade, as given by equation 4.3, cannot be zero unless the trading strategy is 100 percent profitable. Since in practice we are always dealing with trading systems with P < 100, we are allowed to divide equation 4.8 by the average losing trade:

$$\frac{\overline{W}}{\overline{L}}P - (1 - P) > 0 \tag{4.10}$$

Next, we define the ratio of average winning to average losing trade, R_{WL}, as follows:

$$R_{WL} = \frac{\overline{W}}{\overline{L}} \tag{4.11}$$

By combining equations 4.10 and 4.11 and after solving for P we obtain the result:

$$P > \frac{1}{1 + R_{WL}} \tag{4.12}$$

I call equation 4.12 the *profitability rule*.

Equation 4.12 relates the minimum profitability required to generate a net profit, over a period of time T, to the ratio of average winning to average losing trade calculated over the same period. If, instead of the greater-than sign in 4.12, the equality sign is used, that denotes the profitability, or success rate, of break-even performance, assuming commissions and other fees are included in the calculation of the average win and average loss. Thus, the minimum profitability of a trading system so that it breaks even over a period of time T is given by

$$P = \frac{1}{1 + R_{WL}} \tag{4.13}$$

	Minimum Profitability as a Function of the Ratio of Average Win to Average Loss
TABLE 4.1	

R_{WL}	Minimum P ($\times 100$)
10	9.09%
5	16.67%
2	33.33%
1	50.00%
0.5	66.67%
0.25	80.00%
0.125	88.88%

Table 4.1 shows the minimum profitability for various values of R_{WL} computed using equation 4.13. It is clear that there is an inverse relation between the profitability P and the ratio R_{WL}. As R_{WL} increases, the minimum profitability of a trading system required for break-even performance decreases. Thus, in regard to the value of the R_{WL} parameter, the following two observations can be made:

1. Trading systems with low R_{WL} values must have high profitability, which implies a much larger number of winning trades than losing trades.
2. Trading systems with high R_{WL} values can sustain lower profitability; thus they can generate fewer winning trades than losing trades and still be profitable.

Equation 4.13 can be solved for the minimum R_{WL} value required in order for a trading system to maintain the minimum profitability P:

$$R_{WL} = \frac{1-P}{P} \qquad (4.14)$$

Equation 4.14 can be used to estimate the minim risk/reward ratio required given the minimum (break-even) profitability P.

Table 4.2 shows some examples of the minimum required value of the parameter R_{WL} for various values of profitability P, computed using equation 4.14. It is clear from the table that the profitability increases as the value of the parameter R_{WL} decreases.

TABLE 4.2	Minimum Required Ratio of Average Win to Average Loss as a Function of Profitability
Minimum P (×1100)	**Required R_{WL}**
20	4
30	2.33
50	1
67	0.49
70	0.42
75	0.33
90	0.11

THE FUNDAMENTAL LAW OF TRADING STRATEGIES

Equation 4.12, the profitability rule, is an expression of the minimum profitability required in order for a trading system's equity performance to break even over a time period T, as a function of the ratio of average winning to average losing trade R_{WL} calculated over the same period. This equation is useful in terms of obtaining a lower bound on profitability P, but it does not tell us anything about obtaining a desired profit factor P_f. The profit factor is defined as the ratio of the amount of winning trades divided by the amount of losing trades. This parameter is probably the most important to consider when designing and evaluating a trading system.

Experienced trading system designers know that it is the profit factor that ultimately tells us whether a trading system performs, regardless of the values of profitability and average win to average loss ratio. In other words, the profit factor is a measure of the potential of a trading system to generate profit besides just being profitable. Traders prefer systems with a profit factor at least equal to 2, meaning that the amount of winners is twice as large as the amount of losers over a period of time. Intraday trading systems tend to have lower profit factors and trend-following systems usually have much higher values. Short-term, position, and swing trading systems fall somewhere in between regarding the values of the profit factor that can be achieved in that time frame. In general, the higher the profit factor, the better the system performance.

Traders often get the impression that the profit factor is an ad-hoc measure, again by virtue of the vague and often confusing way these topics have been covered in the trading literature by and large. On the contrary, this important parameter is hidden in equation 4.1 and it is revealed when we divide through the equation by the second term, the sum of losing trades (always a positive quantity in reality), and then rearrange to yield:

$$P_f = \frac{\sum_T W}{\sum_T L} > 1 \tag{4.15}$$

Equation 4.15 is the definition of the profit factor P_f, and this parameter must be greater than one in order for a trading system to be profitable. By using equations 4.2, 4.3, 4.5, and 4.11, equation 4.15 becomes

$$P_f = \frac{N_W}{N - N_W} R_{WL} \tag{4.16}$$

Now, we can divide both the numerator and denominator of equation 4.16 by $N > 0$ and use the definition of profitability P of equation 4.7 to get:

$$P_f = \frac{P}{1 - P} R_{WL} \tag{4.17}$$

Equation 4.17 is an expression for the profit factor as a function of the profitability and ratio of average winning to average losing trade. This equation tells us that the three parameters involved are connected by a unique functional relationship. This implies that given any two of the parameters, the third is uniquely determined. Solving equation 4.17 for profitability P yields the final result:

$$P = \frac{P_f}{P_f + R_{WL}} \tag{4.18}$$

Equation 4.18 is more general than equation 4.12, because it is an expression of the profitability P as a function of the profit factor P_f *and* ratio of average winning to average losing trade R_{WL}. I call equation 4.18 the *fundamental law of trading strategies*. Given the expected profit factor and the expected ratio of average winning to average losing trade, this fundamental law determines the profitability of the system. Alternatively, for a desired profit factor and an expected ratio of average winning to average losing trade, the minimum profitability P of a trading system must satisfy the following:

$$P \geq \frac{P_f}{P_f + R_{WL}} \tag{4.19}$$

Table 4.3 shows values of the minimum profitability, calculated using equation 4.18, for various values of the ratio of average winning to average losing trade and profit factor. When comparing the values of P in this

	Minimum Profitability as a Function of	
TABLE 4.3	the Ratio of Average Winning to Average	
	Losing Trade and Profit Factor	

R_{WL}	Profit Factor P_f	Minimum P ($\times$100)
10	1	9.09%
5	1	16.67%
2	1.5	42.85%
1	2	66.67%
0.5	2	80.00%
0.25	2	88.90%
0.125	1	88.88%

table with those displayed in Table 4.1, we can immediately notice that increased values of the profit factor demand increased profitability. For instance, for a profit factor of 1 and a ratio of average winning to average losing trade equal to 1, the required minimum profitability shown in Table 4.1 is 50 percent. If the profit factor is doubled to 2, the minimum profitability is increased to 66.67 percent, as shown in Table 4.3.

Table 4.4 illustrates the influence of the profit factor on trading system profitability by considering a constant ratio of average win to average loss, R_{WL}, equal to 1. It may be seen that a 100 percent increase in the profit factor from 1.50 to 3.00 increases the minimum profitability value from 60 to 75 percent, which is a 25 percent increase and very hard to obtain in practice. Another interesting observation is that when either the ratio of average winning to average losing trade is very small or the profit factor is

	Minimum Profitability
	as a Function of Profit
	Factor for a Ratio of
TABLE 4.4	Average Winning to
	Average Losing Trade
	Set Equal to 1

P_f	Minimum P ($\times$100)
1.00	50.00%
1.25	55.56%
1.50	60.00%
1.75	63.64%
2.00	66.67%
2.50	71.43%
3.00	75.00%

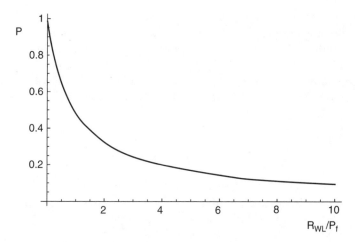

FIGURE 4.1 Graph of profitability P versus the parameter R_{WL}/P_f.

large, the minimum profitability gets asymptotically close to 100 percent. This can be seen from equation 4.18 after dividing the numerator and the denominator by the profit factor P_f:

$$P = \frac{1}{1 + \frac{R_{WL}}{P_f}} \qquad (4.20)$$

It can be seen from equation 4.20 that as P_f gets very large or R_{WL} gets very small, the value of the minimum profitability P approaches 1 ($\sim$100% required success rate), because the ratio R_{WL}/P_f is very small as compared to the number 1 in both cases.

The ratio R_{WL}/P_f can be considered as a new parameter so that the profitability can be plotted against it. Figure 4.1 shows a graph of the profitability P as a function of the ratio R_{WL}/P_f. It is clear from the graph that the demand for higher profitability rises fast as the value of the ratio drops below 4 and is comparatively flat for all practical purposes for values of the ratio above 4. This happens, of course, due to the inverse functional relationship between the two variables.

EFFECT OF COMMISSIONS ON PROFITABILITY

The general form of the profitability rule given by equation 4.18 considers trading commissions implicitly. This means that in order to use the equation any commissions paid must be included in the calculation of the ratio of average win to average loss. Subtracting commissions from winning trades and adding commissions to losing trades can achieve this. Next, we will study the effect of trading commissions on profitability explicitly, by defining C as the round-trip commission charged per trade. We will thus assume that commission charges are not included in the calculation of the ratio of average win to average loss. Equation 4.15 can be modified to include commissions as follows:

$$P_f = \frac{N_W \overline{W} - N_W C}{N_L \overline{L} + N_L C} \tag{4.21}$$

Next, we divide both the numerator and denominator of equation 4.21 by the product of the number of losing trades times the average losing trade (a positive number) to obtain

$$P_f = \frac{\frac{N_W \overline{W}}{N_L \overline{L}} - \frac{N_W C}{N_L \overline{L}}}{1 + \frac{C}{\overline{L}}} \tag{4.22}$$

We now define the commission factor C_f as the ratio of the round-trip commission C to the average losing trade:

$$C_f = \frac{C}{\overline{L}} \tag{4.23}$$

By using equations 4.5, 4.11, and 4.21, equation 4.23 becomes

$$P_f = \frac{\frac{N_W}{N - N_W}(R_{WL} - C_f)}{1 + C_f} \tag{4.24}$$

It may be seen immediately from equation 4.24 that the commission factor C_f is subtracted from the ratio of average win to average loss R_{WL}, and this should have been expected. Next, by using the definition of profitability given by equation 4.7, equation 4.26 becomes

$$P_f = \frac{\frac{P}{P - 1}(R_{WL} - C_f)}{1 + C_f} \tag{4.25}$$

Solving equation 4.25 for the profitability P, we obtain the result:

$$P = \frac{P_f}{P_f + \frac{R_{WL} - C_f}{1 + C_f}} \tag{4.26}$$

We can again see that if the commission factor C_f is set to zero, equation 4.26 reduces to equation 4.18, the profitability rule. Commissions paid affects the term related to the ratio of average winning to average losing trade, by reducing it to a new ratio R'_{WL} equal to

$$R'_{WL} = \frac{R_{WL} - C_f}{1 + C_f} \tag{4.27}$$

Now it can be seen from equation 4.26 that as the value of the commission factor C_f increases the required profitability also increases. If C_f is kept low, then the ratio of average winning to average losing trade is not affected and the profitability P can be approximated by equation 4.18. The profitability rule, when adjusted for commissions, reveals a disturbing reality of trading strategies: One way to keep C_f low is to increase the average losing trade, as can be seen from equation 4.23. But this also requires a proportional increase in the average winning trade to maintain the value of the R_{WL} ratio at acceptable levels and to minimize the demand for higher profitability. But when one attempts to increase the average winning trade, the effectiveness of the strategy decreases because more trades turn to losers due to price volatility. The net result is a reduction in the number of winning trades, effectively causing the actual profitability to decrease. The commission burden on trading system design and its effects are more pronounced in intraday trading time frames and, to a lesser extent, in short-term trading time frames.

In practice, instead of using equation 4.27, an approximation can be used of the following form:

$$R'_{WL} = \alpha R_{WL} \tag{4.28}$$

where α is a constant that takes values in the range 0 to 1. Low values of the constant result in higher minimum profitability for a desired profit factor and expected ratio of average winning to average losing trade. The approximate form of the profitability rule as a result of using equation 4.28 is then

$$P = \frac{P_f}{P_f + \alpha R_{WL}} \tag{4.29}$$

where P is the minimum profitability required to achieve a profit factor P_f, given that the ratio of average win to average loss R_{WL} can be estimated (excluding commissions), and α is a factor that accounts for commission, slippage, and other random effects that impact trade execution and bottom line-performance. In the case of intraday trading a value for α in the range 0.5–0.7 is recommended depending on the trading frequency of the particular strategy used. In short-term trading time frames, values in the range 0.7–0.9 may be used. The situation for longer-term trading is more complicated, and while the choice for the appropriate value of α may depend on

TABLE 4.5	Effect of Commissions on Minimum Profitability as a Function of the Ratio of Average Winning to Average Losing Trade (profit factor = 2)		
R_{WL}	P ($\times 100$) $\alpha = 1$	P ($\times 100$) $\alpha = 0.7$	% Change
10	16.67%	22.22%	33.3%
5	28.57%	36.36%	27.3%
2	50.00%	58.82%	17.6%
1	66.56%	74.07%	11.3%
0.5	80.00%	85.10%	6.4%
0.25	88.88%	91.95%	3.5%

the trading strategy used, as a general rule, it can be set to 1 for all practical purposes when the expected profitability of the trading system is 50 percent or more.

Table 4.5 illustrates the effect of commissions on minimum profitability for different values of the ratio of average winning to average losing trade and for a profit factor equal to 2 and two different values of α. It can be seen that for high values of R_{WL} the percent change in the minimum profitability, for a constant profit factor, is larger. This can be misleading because in practice it is much harder to come up with ways to increase an already-high profitability of a trading strategy than to increase a low profitability. For instance, increasing the profitability of a trading system from 80 to 85.10 percent is much more difficult in practice than from 50 to 55 percent.

The constant α in equation 4.29 can be assigned values that take into account factors that affect trading system performance, such as slippage, partial fills, and bad executions. Equation 4.29 is very important for understanding some of the tradeoffs present in the design of trading systems. Although mathematically it is a very simple formula, it is very fundamental and every trader should study it carefully and understand its hidden implications for the performance of trading systems operating in different time frames.

PROFITABILITY AND TRADING TIME FRAMES

Short-term and intraday trading systems usually have much lower R_{WL} values than do trend-following systems. The typical range of the ratio of average winning to average losing trade for short-term or intraday trading systems is 0.25 to 2. Trend-following systems demand values much greater than 2, usually in the range 4–6. The reason for this fundamental difference

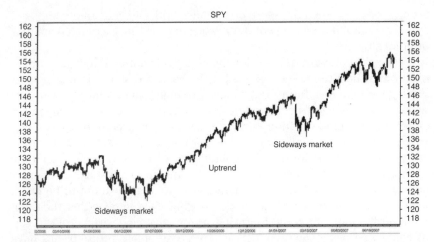

FIGURE 4.2 Sideways markets followed by uptrends in SPY daily prices.
Source: APS Automatic Pattern Search.

is that in short-term and intraday trading, the profit target and stop-loss levels are mainly dictated by price volatility. In the case of trend-following systems, the objective is by design to minimize losses that occur during sideways or choppy markets and maximize the profits made during price trends.

As an example, Figure 4.2 is a daily chart of the SPY exchange-traded fund and shows periods of sideways-moving prices followed by uptrends. The objective of a trend-following system in this particular case would be to minimize losses during sideways moves and maximize profits during uptrends. This results in higher R_{WL} values since the average win is large and the average loss is kept as low as possible. In relation to the profitability rule, in intraday and short-term trading systems it is highly likely that future R_{WL} values will closely match the values determined during back testing. This is because in these trading time frames, the methods used to generate exit signals depend mainly on price volatility. The result is that R_{WL} values stay in a range over the longer term due to volatility mean-reversion. This is especially true when using profit targets and stop-losses based on a fixed amount or number of points.

Therefore, if the profitability of a trading system is maintained above the minimum value, as dictated by the profitability rule, the system will always perform according to expectations. This is because, according to equation 4.18, if R_{WL} remains within a tight range, the required profitability P to realize a desired profit factor P_f will not vary significantly. Thus, one may think in an inverse way, and take appropriate steps during

trading system design to assure compliance with the constraints imposed
by the profitability rule. One of these steps may be the use of fixed amount
or point stops.

The situation with trend-following systems is not as simple as with intraday and short-term ones, as was briefly discussed above. In longer-term
trading time frames, future R_{WL} values are highly uncertain and can vary
widely from the values obtained during back testing. This can happen because the magnitude of future price trends, as compared to past ones, can
vary greatly. At the same time, the performance of position-exiting methods used depends on future price volatility. Because neither the magnitude
of future trends nor price volatility can be known in advance, as a consequence, the actual values of the parameter R_{WL} may turn out to be much
lower than those obtained from back testing. This implies that the minimum profitability of a trend-following system given a desired profit factor,
as calculated using equation 4.18, will increase unless future trends have
an equal or greater magnitude compared with the past and price volatility
remains the same or is lower. This is an outcome of the stochastic nature
of the profitability rule in the case of trend-following systems due to the
parameter R_{WL} being a random variable.

The profitability rule provides this insight based on its quantitative content and it exposes some difficulties in designing profitable trend-following
systems. The most important implication of the profitability rule in the case
of trend-following trading systems is that a much higher profitability may
be required than the one determined based on historical R_{WL} values to protect against future variations in the ratio of average win to average loss.
This imposes additional constraints in the design of trend-following systems, which must be robust enough to account for adverse future market conditions resulting in much lower R_{WL} values. This realization challenges the common notion that trend-following systems can have much
lower profitability than short-term or intraday systems. Designing a trend-
following trading system that can stay profitable for an extended period of
time is a truly challenging task and the profitability rule sheds light on the
fundamental nature of these difficulties.

Another way of dealing with the constraints imposed on trading system design by the profitability rule is by attempting to limit its stochastic
nature as much as possible. Since the profitability of a trading strategy cannot be fixed in advance but only measured empirically, a trading system
designer should try to minimize the randomness of the R_{WL} parameter. It
appears that the only way this can be done effectively is by implementing strategies that result in a constant ratio of average winning to average
losing trade over extended periods of time. This can be accomplished, for
example, if profit target and stop-loss levels are based on fixed amounts
or points.

Although in reality losing trades tend to be larger than expected due to slippage and occasional adverse gaps in prices, these effects are counterbalanced in the longer term by comparable variations in winning trades. What the profitability rule tells us is that in order to minimize the uncertainty in trading system performance and keep the required minimum profitability as low as possible, one must try to minimize the uncertainty in the value of the ratio of average winning to average losing trade, R_{WL}. According to this interpretation of the profitability rule and given the fact that trend following has inherent uncertainty, it appears that short-term and intraday trading time frames offer potential for a more robust performance if certain conditions are met. This contradicts another notion that longer-term investment strategies have an advantage over short-term strategies. Given that trend following requires in addition discipline for holding open positions for an extended period of time, this may be an explanation for the popularity of short-term and intraday trading.

The practical application of the profitability rule in short-term and intraday trading dictates using profit target and stop-loss levels based on the trade entry price. In this case the profitability rule, as expressed by equation 4.27, can be approximated by

$$P = \frac{P_f}{P_f + \alpha T/S} \qquad (4.30)$$

where T is the profit target and S the stop-loss, measured as fixed amounts or in points. This may even work in the case where T and S are fixed percentages of the entry price. Thus, in this way the ratio of average winning to average losing trade R_{WL} in equation 4.29 is approximated in equation 4.30 by the ratio of profit target to stop-loss, T/S.

Equation 4.30, when solved for T/S, provides a lower-bound estimate of the ratio of profit target to stop-loss required for a desired profit factor and expected profitability:

$$\frac{T}{S} = \frac{P_f}{\alpha} \cdot \frac{1 - P}{P} \qquad (4.31)$$

As an example, for a profit factor equal to 2, an expected profitability of 60 percent, and α set equal to 0.7, the minimum value of the ratio T/S is, according to equation 4.30:

$$\frac{T}{S} = \frac{2}{0.7} \cdot \frac{1 - 0.6}{0.6} = 1.9 \qquad (4.32)$$

Therefore, the profit target should be roughly double the stop-loss in order to obtain the desired profit factor given the expected profitability of 60 percent.

Equation 4.30 offers an explanation as to why scalpers, who are subjected to occasional large drawdowns, aim for the impossible. If the profit factor is equal to 1, which denotes a break-even condition, for a typical T/S ratio realized by these traders equal to 0.4, and $\alpha = 1$ (an ideal situation), the minimum profitability required is

$$P_{min} = \frac{1}{1 + 0.4} = 0.714 \tag{4.33}$$

Equation 4.33 indicates that a scalper must achieve a success rate of 71.4 percent, which means slightly better than 7 winners in every 10 trades on average, just to break even, commissions and slippage not accounted for. I hope that this result will convince some scalpers to reconsider their trading style and escape their destiny, which is a redistribution of their capital in the zero-sum game of trading.

EXAMPLES

The solutions to the following questions demonstrate the use of the profitability rule.

Question 1: A trader of 10-yr note futures realizes a profit of $1,000 in each winning trade and a loss of $400 in each losing trade. The trader is profitable 6 times out of 10 on the average over the longer term. (a) What is the trader's profit factor? (b) By what factor does this trader exceed the minimum profitability required for a break-even performance?

Solution:

(a) First we calculate the ratio of average winning to average losing trade as follows:

$$R_{WL} = \$1,000/\$400 = 2.5$$

Using equation 4.17, we calculate the profit factor P_f:

$$P_f = (0.6 \times 2.5)/(1.0 - 0.6) = 3.75$$

Thus, the sum of winning trades will be 3.75 times the sum of losing trades over a sufficiently long period of time.

(b) The minimum profitability is found by applying equation 4.12:

$$P_{min} = 100/(1 + 2.5) = 28.57\%$$

The trader's profitability P exceeds P_{min} by a factor equal to

$$100 \times (60\% - 28.57\%)/28.57\% = 110\%$$

Question 2: Trader A is as profitable as trader B but trader B has twice the ratio of average winning to average losing trade of trader A. How do their profit factors compare?
Solution:

$$\text{For } trader \text{ A} : P_{fA} = [P/(P-1)] \times R_{WLA}$$
$$\text{Similarly for trader B} : P_{fB} = [P/(P-1)] \times R_{WLB}$$

Dividing P_{fA} by P_{fB} we get

$$P_{fA}/P_{fB} = R_{WLA}/R_{WLB}$$

Since $R_{WLB} = 2 \times R_{WLA}$ we get the expected result:

$$P_{fA}/P_{fB} = 1/2$$

Thus, the profit factor of trader A is half that of trader B. If profitability stays constant, any increase in the ratio of average winning to average losing trade results in a comparable increase of the profit factor.

Question 3: A trend follower expects to achieve profitability P of 20 percent and has a stop-loss of $500. How large should his average winner trade be so that he will end up with a profit factor equal to 2?
Solution: From equation 4.14 we obtain

$$R_{WL} = [(1-P)/P] \times P_f = [(1-0.2)/0.2] \times 2.0 = 8.0$$
$$\text{But, } R_{WL} = \text{avg. winner/avg. loser} = \text{avg. winner/\$500} = 8.0$$
$$\text{Then, avg. winner} = \$4,000$$

Thus, the average winner must be at least $4,000 to maintain a profit factor of 2.0 when the profitability is 20 percent and the average loser is $500.

The profitability rule derived in this chapter provides a rigorous way of assessing the limitations and constraints present in the design of trading systems for use in different trading time frames. It also provides a means for estimating quite accurately some important trading system performance parameters based on actual measurements. When profitability is combined with sound risk and money management, which is the subject of the next chapter, then the task of developing winning systematic trading methodologies becomes more realistic and highly rewarding.

CHAPTER 5

Risk and Money Management

Systematic traders spend considerable time and resources in developing trading systems. A trading system that generates profitable entry signals in the time frame considered is necessary for success but is not sufficient. Necessity and sufficiency toward success are achieved only when the signals generated by a system with acceptable historical testing and actual trading records are combined with proper risk and money management.

It is important to understand that any risk and money management method used must be an integral part of the trading system design and part of the historical testing phase. Some technical traders attempt to implement complicated risk and money management techniques that are not part of the model used to test a trading system. However, the application of any risk and money management method alters the dynamics of a trading system and actual trading performance may vary significantly from back-testing results that do not consider the method.

Often, trading system developers attempt to maximize the equity performance produced by a historical back test by increasing open position size using realized profits. It is understood that such methods will work well for trading systems with profitable historical back-test results and an equity curve that is increasing. During actual trading, however, adding to position size may be the cause of a disaster, especially where the trading system does not perform as expected and the equity curve turns south. The situation is even worse in the case of "fitted" or "optimized" systems. Any aggressive risk and money management technique applied to such systems can be hazardous to actual performance rather than improving it.

Furthermore, treatments of the subject of position sizing in books, magazines, or web sites fall under two major categories: The first category deals with specific strategies often presented with limited or no testing and lacking theoretical justification. Nevertheless, some of the strategies are realistic and can be applied to actual trading. The second category involves complicated strategies that are unrealistic to apply.

Some books on risk and money management present theoretical treatments of the subject and are stuffed with mathematical equations, and the concepts are beyond the grasp of the average trader. The main problem that traders face when trying to find their way thought this information maze is an apparent lack of a direct connection between some of the risk and money management strategies proposed and the realities of their particular trading system.

Traders should always remember that a risk and money management strategy is useful only if a system with a winning bias, or positive expected gain, is available to start with. Also, systematic trading makes sense only if the necessary discipline and skills are there to follow the signals of a system and execute the appropriate entry/exit orders. When a trading system with acceptable performance is available and the discipline and required skills are there, proper risk management and position sizing can make the difference between a mediocre, or even negative, performance and spectacular returns.

In this chapter, I discuss basic but very effective risk and money management methods that are known to work and are being used by many successful traders. I start the discussion with the determination of the minimum capital required to trade a system, which is a basic first step in risk management that many traders tend to skip. Then, I present some very simple formulas for calculating trading capital requirements and risk percent. Finally, I approach position sizing through a very effective method and derive formulas that can be used to implement it.

THE PROBABILITY OF RUIN

An important part of risk and money management—and often the most overlooked—is the determination of the starting capital required to trade a system so that the probability of ruin is minimized. Novice traders often underestimate the importance of starting capital requirements because they think that it suffices merely to have a profitable trading system in order to accumulate wealth. There are random short-term effects, however, that can cause total depletion of trading capital even if the trading system performs according to expectations over the longer-term. These random effects may contribute to clusters of consecutive losing trades and to a large equity drawdown that cannot be sustained.

In order to understand the hazardous effect consecutive losing trades can have on trading system performance, consider as an example two traders, Peter and Paul, who use the same trading system. Peter risks 2 percent of his starting capital amount in each trade while Paul risks 5 percent. We assume that both traders start at the same time and the system generates 20 consecutive losers. In this case, Paul ends up with no money in his trading account whereas Peter's account is reduced by 40 percent. If the trading system turns profitable after the streak of 20 losing trades and generates a large number of consecutive winners, then Peter may be in a position to recover the loss and even make a profit. However, Paul is unable to trade unless he adds more funds to his account.

Table 5.1 shows a few examples of the number of consecutive losing trades, denoted as C_L, required to completely wipe out an account of any size as a function of the percentage of the starting capital risked in each trade. The percent risk is assumed to be a constant for all trades.

A typical reaction of an inexperienced trader who risks 4 percent, for example, of his account equity on each trade after looking at Table 4.1 might be: "My system will never generate 25 consecutive losers!"

The bad news is that *probability theory* says otherwise. There is always a finite probability that any trading system with profitability less than 100 percent will generate just the number of consecutive losers required to wipe out an account of any size.

In order to better understand the probability of ruin, let us model a trading system that generates market entry signals as an experiment of tossing a coin. For this purpose, we will equate heads to losing trades and tails to winning trades. Normally, the probability in the case of a fair coin of getting heads or tails is 0.5. We will assume that the trading system is

TABLE 5.1	Number of Consecutive Losers That Will Ruin a Starting Capital of Any Size as a Function of Risk Percent
Percent Risk	C_L
1	100
2	50
3	33
4	25
5	20

more than 50 percent profitable, because there is a bias in the experiment so that the probability of getting heads is smaller than that of getting tails. Let us call the probability of heads p and that of tails $(1 - p)$.

The formula to calculate the probability of getting k heads in n coin tosses, denoted as P(k in n), is known as *Bernoulli Trials* (Papoulis 1965, pp. 57–61):

$$P(k \text{ in } n) = \frac{n!}{k!(n - k)!} p^k (1 - p)^{n-k} \tag{5.1}$$

where (!) stands for the factorial operator:

$$n! = 1 \times 2 \times 3 \times \ldots \times n \tag{5.2}$$

By definition: $0! = 1$. As an example, $4! = 1 \times 2 \times 3 \times 4 = 24$.

Let us now apply equation 5.1 to calculate the probability of getting 25 consecutive losers in a total of 25 trades, modeled as coin tosses in our example. Thus, k and n both equal 25. We assume that the trading system has profitability 70 percent, which means that $(1 - p) = 0.7$ and $p = 0.3$. After plugging all the parameter values into equation 5.1, we obtain

$$P(25 \text{ in } 25) = \frac{25!}{25!(25 - 25)!} (0.3)^{25} (0.7)^0$$

or

$$P(25 \text{ in } 25) = 8.47 \times 10^{-14}$$

The value of the probability calculated above is very low but it is finite. But all losing trades need not come in a row, as in the above example. Out of the many possibilities that exist, it suffices getting 10 consecutive losing trades, followed by two consecutive winning trades and then 10 more consecutive losing trades, followed by three consecutive winning trades and finally 10 more consecutive losing trades.

In the following example, we increase the number of losing trades to 30 while adding 5 winning trades and we also assume that the sizes of winning and losing trades are equal, for simplicity. Thus, in a total of 35 trades, 5 winners compensate for the loss of 5 losers and the net result is 25 losers. The probability of this scenario happening, according to formula 5.1, is equal to

$$P(30 \text{ in } 35) = \frac{35!}{30!(35 - 30)!} (0.3)^{30} (0.7)^5 \cong 1.123 \times 10^{-11}$$

The probability of getting 30 losers in a total of 35 trades using a system that is 70 percent profitable is three orders of magnitude less (a factor of 1,000) than in the previous example of 25 consecutive losing trades in a row. Although the probability is still very low, if a trader is "lucky" enough he can hit the jackpot and get ruined before a turnaround in system performance occurs. As an example, the odds of getting 6 out of 59 numbers in New York State Lotto are 1 in 45,057,474. This means that the probability of any random pick of six numbers to win is equal to 2.22×10^{-8}. Although this is also a very small probability, there are occasionally winners even with a single lottery ticket.

As became evident from the previous examples, there is always a finite small probability of ruin even when care is taken to keep risk exposure low. Thus, trading systems with high profitability and low percent risk per trade have a very low but still finite probability of ruin. The low probability turns into a certain event if the system becomes unprofitable at some point. The number of maximum consecutive losing trades that is calculated during the back testing of a trading system provides no indication of what may occur in the future. Therefore, in order to minimize the probability of ruin, the percentage of the account equity risked in each trade must be minimized.

However, lower risk percent implies lower reward, which is an expected tradeoff, and the task becomes one of figuring out the optimum risk for a given market and trading system. Since future market conditions cannot be known in advance and actual trading system performance cannot be predicted but only empirically measured, experienced traders limit the percent risk to no more than 1 to 2 percent of their account equity or current bankroll. The tradeoff is that at those low levels of risk there is a demand for a large trading account. Novice traders, often misled by ads claiming, for example, that a $500 account grew to $100,000 in a few months, underestimate the implications that proper risk and money management has for trading account size. Ignorance in the trading business results in disastrous financial consequences.

THE FUNDAMENTAL LAW OF RISK AND MONEY MANAGEMENT

One of the primary tasks of every trader who wants to survive the zero-sum game of trading must be the determination of the starting capital required for a particular trading system. This requires determining the percentage of equity to risk on each trade in order to minimize the probability of ruin in a rigorous and quantitative way. Instead, most novice traders start backwards, by opening an account with what they can afford, and then risking as much as possible, even all of it, in each trade, hoping they will be lucky and a streak of winners will come their way before a streak of losers does. We all know the results of such actions and the reality of markets. For most people, the reality is that a streak of losers will always come before a streak of winners does and will be enough to ruin their account.

The account equity, percent risk, and amount risked in each trade are related by the following equation, which I call the *fundamental law of risk and money management*:

$$M = \frac{S}{R} \qquad (5.3)$$

where M is the trading account equity, S is the amount risked per trade, and R is the percent risk.

Trading Capital Requirements

Probably the most important use of equation 5.3 is in determining the starting trading capital M so that a desired risk percent R can be maintained based on a fixed amount S risked per trade. Table 5.2 shows examples of starting trading capital values for various values of risk percent and amount risked. For instance, for a risk percent equal to 0.02, or 2 percent, and for an amount at risk equal to $2,000 per trade, the starting capital requirement is $100,000, according to equation 5.3.

As we can see in Table 5.2, the starting trading capital is inversely proportional to percent risk and directly proportional to the amount risked. Often, the amount risked is not a parameter that can be set independently

TABLE 5.2 Starting Trading Capital Requirements

Risk Percent (%)	Amount Risked ($)	Starting Capital ($)	Number of Consecutive Losers for a 50% Drop in Starting Capital
1.00	500	50,000	
	1,000	100,000	
	2,000	200,000	50
	5,000	500,000	
	10,000	1,000,000	
2.00	500	25,000	
	1,000	50,000	
	2,000	100,000	25
	5,000	250,000	
	10,000	500,000	
5.00	500	10,000	
	1,000	20,000	10
	2,000	40,000	

of the trading method used. In that case, the values this parameter can assume are ultimately dictated by position size and price volatility. As the amount risked is decreased for a given position size, the profitability of a trading system decreases because fewer entry signals can turn to winners. This occurs because stop-loss levels must be set closer to the entry price to limit losses. Thus, the starting capital requirement can be estimated only after a trading system is properly analyzed and the effects of different values of percent risk on equity performance are studied.

As an example, in the case of a short-term trading system for crude oil futures, after careful back testing and analysis it was determined that it can achieve acceptable profitability with an amount risked per trade and per contract equal to $500. In addition, the percent risk is 2 percent of the starting capital. Plugging these values into equation 5.3 yields $25,000 for the value of the starting capital:

$$M = \frac{S}{R} = \frac{\$500}{0.02} = \$25,000$$

The above calculation means that when the trader starts using his system and places the first trade, the risk percent will not be equal to his desired value of 2 percent of his account equity unless the starting capital is equal to $25,000. This is because the system risks $500 on each trade. Now, if the account equity increases to $50,000 due to accumulated profits, the trader can increase position size by adding another contract and the risk percent will remain at the 2 percent level.

Trading on Margin

In order to use equation 5.3, one must make the assumption that the amount risked per trade is known in advance. Some day and short-term trading systems use a constant value for the amount risked per trade; others do not. For example, some short-term bond futures traders risk one full point ($1,000) per trade and intraday traders of the mini-size S&P 500 contract use a fixed number of ticks, corresponding to a fixed dollar amount. This approach is common with futures trading, but in the case of equity trading, some traders prefer to risk a variable amount based on a percentage of the entry price. The amount risked per trade is not known in advance in trading systems that use exit signals generated by indicators.

In addition, equation 5.3 does not take into account margin requirements; thus, it may underestimate trading capital requirements. Use of leverage can impose additional burdens on the starting trading capital requirements and the equation needs to be modified to account for such cases. In order to tackle this problem, we will consider a more general case that takes into account margin requirements. To start with, we note that the maximum drawdown per contract in the case of futures or forex trading in conjunction with the margin requirement per contract determines the minimum starting trading capital per contract that is required in order to avoid liquidation. In the case of stock trading, the situation is slightly different.

Futures and Forex Trading

In order to better understand how trading capital requirements are determined in the case of trading futures or forex on margin, we start with the following definitions:

M_f is the starting trading capital requirement per contract.

D_R is the maximum historical drawdown per contract.

f is a safety factor.

G is the margin deposit per contract.

Based on these definitions, the formula for calculating the starting trading capital requirement per contract is

$$M_f = G + f \cdot D_R \tag{5.4}$$

As an example of the application of equation 5.4, consider the case where the maximum drawdown per contract is equal to \$10,000 and the margin per contract is equal to \$2,000. Then, for f set equal to 1, the starting trading capital requirement per contract is calculated using equation 5.4 to be \$12,000. If the safety factor f is set equal to 1.5, the starting capital value increases to \$18,000.

Since only historical or past values of the drawdown are available, the safety factor f is included in equation 5.4 to account for a possible future increase in the drawdown.

After combining equations 5.3 and 5.4, we get the following equation for the percent risk R:

$$R = \frac{S}{G + f \cdot D_R} \tag{5.5}$$

Equation 5.5 is an expression of the percent risk per contract R as a function of amount risked per trade S, the margin G, and the maximum drawdown D_R. A safety factor f is also included to account for future increases in drawdown.

As an example of the use of equation 5.5, the following values are considered:

Amount risked per trade and per contract S = $1,000.

Drawdown per contract D_R = $10,000.

Margin per contract G = $2,000.

Safety factor f = 2 (accounts for a possible twofold increase in future drawdown values).

Plugging in the values from equation 5.5 yields

$$R = 1,000/(2,000 + 2.0 \times 10,000) = 0.04545 \text{ or } R = 4.54\%$$

The risk per trade R is 4.54 percent in this example. The starting capital requirement is

$$M = 2,000 + 2.0 \times 10,000 = \$22,000$$

If this level of risk is unacceptable, then either equation 5.3 must be used to calculate the starting trading capital for the acceptable level of risk or the amount risked per trade must be lowered. In the present example, if the acceptable maximum risk per trade is 2 percent, then according to equation 5.3 the starting trading capital must be equal to $50,000, which is more than double the $22,000 figure obtained earlier. The larger of the two values must be used in order to maintain the acceptable level of percent risk. Lowering the percent risk in this example made a big difference in the size of the starting trading capital. However, the decrease in the probability of ruin from an increase in capitalization requirements is often enormous. In the case of a 4.54 percent risk, it will take about 11 consecutive losing trades for a 50 percent drop in equity, whereas for a 2 percent risk per trade, 25 losing trades are required.

Stock Trading

In order to better understand how trading capital requirements are determined in the case of stock trading, we start with the following definitions:

M_e is the initial trading capital.

S is the amount risked per trade.

R is the percent risk.

f is a safety factor.

g is the margin multiplier (leverage) factor.

Based on these definitions, the formula for the initial trading capital becomes

$$M_e = \frac{gS}{R} \tag{5.6}$$

It may be seen that if the margin multiplier g is set to 1, equation 5.6 reduces to equation 5.3.

For example, if the amount risked in each trade is \$300, the percent risk is 2 percent, the margin multiplier factor is equal to 2 (amount loaned is equal to cash value of the account), and f is set equal to 1, then according to equation 5.6 the initial trading capital is calculated as follows:

$$M_e = (2 \times \$300)/0.02 = \$30,000$$

Note that the factor g in equation 5.6 causes a proportional decrease in percent risk R so that that the equivalent percent risk R/g results in the starting trading capital requirement increasing by a comparable factor.

In addition, in the case of stock trading on margin, the starting trading cash account must be at least equal to the maximum drawdown D_R multiplied by a safety factor. After setting M_e/g equal to f times D_R in equation 5.6 and then solving for the percent risk R we obtain

$$\frac{M_e}{g} = f \cdot D_R \Rightarrow M_e = g \cdot f \cdot D_R = \frac{g \cdot S}{R} \Rightarrow R = \frac{S}{f \cdot D_R} \tag{5.7}$$

As an example, consider a stock trading system that has a maximum drawdown of \$10,000 and \$100 is risked on each trade. The leverage is 4 times the starting trading capital. The safety factor f is set equal to 1.0. The percent risk R for a starting trading capital M_e equal to the maximum drawdown of \$10,000 is

$$R = (4 \times \$100)/(1.0 \times 10,000) = 0.04 \text{ or } R = 4.0\% \tag{5.8}$$

With a percent risk of 4 percent it will take about 25 consecutive losers to exhaust the trading capital. In reality, brokers may liquidate the account much earlier due to insufficient funds to cover maintenance margin of open positions.

In equations 5.4 and 5.6, the values of the starting trading capital and risk percent obtained ultimately depend on the magnitude of the safety factor f. Increasing f results in increased starting trading capital but also in reduced performance. Decreasing f results in reduced starting trading capital but also in increased performance. There is no practical method of determining the optimal value of the safety factor f. The optimum value ultimately depends on future drawdown values that are unknown.

A trading system developer must choose a value for f based on experience. For new stock trading systems, a value of f in the range 1.5–3 is recommended. This should act as a guard against an unexpected increase in drawdown.

POSITION SIZING

In this chapter, the fundamental law of risk and money management has been introduced and one of its primary applications was discussed, that of determining the starting capital requirement for trading systems with specific risk parameters. In this section, we will use the law to determine position size given the risk tolerances.

As an example of the application of position sizing, consider a swing trader of U.S. equities. The trading system he uses has a profit target of $1 and a stop-loss of $0.50 and thus risks a predetermined amount per trade because this is what works in his case. The amount risked is equal to 50 cents times the number of shares bought long or sold short, or equivalently, it is equal to the position size times the stop-loss value. The position size in this particular case depends on the percentage of the account equity that the trader is willing to risk in each trade. If, for example, the account equity is $100,000 and the trader is willing to risk 1 percent of that in each trade, then the number of shares times the stop-loss must equal 0.01 × $100,000, which amounts to $1,000.

The proper position size is calculated by dividing the amount risked per trade by the stop-loss value, and in this example the result is $1,000/$0.5, or 2,000 shares. Thus, the trader can buy or sell, depending on whether the trading signal is long or short, 2,000 shares with a stop-loss set equal to half a point. If the stop-loss price is hit, then the loss will equal $0.5 × 2,000, which amounts to $1,000 and, after commissions and possible slippage, very close to the 1 percent of the available capital of $100,000 the trader wishes to risk.

If the stop-loss is expressed as a percentage of the entry price, rather than in points, the same reasoning applies when calculating the number of shares—just the details change slightly—as will be shown later when the mathematical formulas of position sizing are derived.

The above example demonstrated the concept of position sizing based on the risk percent method. This method is also known as *fixed fractional position sizing*. However, some may insist that there are ways to calculate position size using concepts like volatility or optimal bet sizing. The question that naturally arises from such claims is, What purpose will such departures from the simple risk percent method serve?

The objective of the previous example was to calculate position size so that if a trade turns into a loser, the loss will amount to 1 percent, or whatever percentage the trader chooses, of the available equity. The solution obtained is unique in that respect because the equity and risk tolerances are known in advance. Any other method produces results that vary the risk percent in exchange for a promise of increased equity performance in the longer term. It is this departure from the simple and commonsense approach to position-size determination offered by the risk percent method that often creates confusion in the minds of traders, especially when the alternative methods are based on unjustifiable assumptions about the future performance of trading systems.

In essence, some of the proposed alternatives to the risk percent method adjust risk by varying the number of shares bought or sold, and thus the amount risked per trade, using various advanced mathematical concepts and algorithms. One assumption that is commonly made by such methods is that the trading system winning bias will be maintained in the short to medium term. But if this assumption is false and the system experiences an unexpected drawdown while the level of risk is excessive, the result can be a disaster.

Some retail brokers provide tools for calculating the "optimal" position size, or bet size, as part of the functionality of their trading platforms. The number of shares or contracts bought long or sold short when using calculators provided by these platforms is much larger than what would have been obtained using the (fixed) risk percent method employed in the previous example. Some alternative methods by which optimal position sizing is determined are *Optimal-f*, *Kelly formula*, or *fixed ratio position sizing*, to name just a few. They are also designated as *Martingale* or *anti-Martingale* methods after borrowing terminology from probability theory.

Although traders should always try to explore alternative position sizing strategies that maximize growth, they should never use them if the risk percent R that results is higher than what they can tolerate, and especially if the objective of these methods is more that of managing positions than risk. More importantly, some of these alternative optimal methods require input of the values of various trading system performance parameters. Obviously, there is no way to use such methods with newly developed systems, because there is no justification for equating the historical values of the parameters with what will be obtained in the future after using the system in real-time trading. Thus, newly developed systems should employ the risk percent method. A transition to optimal bet sizing should be made only after there is sufficient actual data to show that the system performance parameters are stable enough to guarantee medium- to longer-term growth.

Going into more detail in the derivation and use of optimal position-sizing formulas is beyond the scope of this book, but a few comments will be made here regarding the well-known Kelly formula. Professional gamblers and traders use this formula for position sizing, yet one can find several conflicting opinions in articles and online forums about its proper application, even about the proper meaning and use of the result of the formula.

The Kelly formula is based on the work of John Kelly of Bell Laboratories in the 1950s on the subject of telephone transmission signal-to-noise ratio. A simplified version of the original formula is

$$\text{Kelly\%} = P - [(1 - P)/R_{WL}]$$

where Kelly% is the percentage of capital to risk per trade, and P and R_{WL} are the profitability and ratio of average win to average loss, respectively, as defined in Chapter 4. One can easily notice that the right-hand side of the equation is the expected gain E(g), as given by equation 4.9 of Chapter 4, divided by the average winning trade:

$$\text{Kelly\%} = \frac{E(g)}{\overline{W}} = P - [(1 - P)/R_{WL}]$$

But the expected gain E(g) represents the *edge*, which is how much the trading system is expected to win on average, and the average winning trade is the *odds*, which is the average amount won each time the trading system is profitable. Therefore, the optimal bet size according to the Kelly formula is equal to edge divided by odds. This is also the ratio that maximizes geometric equity growth of a profitable trading system.

In the previous example involving the equity swing trader, no mention was made of the performance parameters of the trading system used. It was just assumed it had a winning bias and the only objective of the simple risk percent position-sizing method was to minimize the risk of ruin. However, an application of the Kelly formula to determine position size aims at maximizing equity growth by maximizing risk and requires the actual values of performance parameters of the trading system and specifically of the following two: the success rate (profitability) and the ratio of average win to average loss. This is a dramatic departure from the risk percent method because of the information that must be available in advance before one can determine position size, but also because of the change of objective.

As mentioned earlier, proper position sizing based on the Kelly formula cannot be applied to newly developed trading systems because the actual values for the two parameters that are used by the formula are not available in that case. But even in the case of systems that have been traded for some time, there is no guarantee that these parameters will remain constant. This is especially true for trend-following systems, as discussed in Chapter 4, in which case the average win to average loss ratio is a random variable because it depends on the magnitude of unknown future trends and future price volatility. Therefore, application of advanced position-sizing methods like the Kelly formula requires continuous reevaluation of system performance parameters, and that imposes an additional burden on a trader in exchange for the promise of better equity performance.

THE RISK PERCENT METHOD

The risk percent position-sizing method, also known as fixed fractional position sizing, calculates position size based on the percentage of equity one is willing to risk. It is a practical method with no theoretical justification for its use other than the fact that it has worked well for so many traders in the past and it is highly recommended. Experienced traders always suggest that no more than 1 to 2 percent of the available account equity should be risked on any trade. In this way, the probability of ruin discussed in the beginning of this chapter is low enough. The risk percent values recommended have been determined by experience and many traders use them because they value experience more than theoretical advice. For the risk percent method to work, the trade exit price must be known in advance. This method does not apply to trading systems that use exit strategies with varying, or unknown in advance, exit price levels.

The formula for the risk percent position-sizing method can be obtained by applying equation 5.3, the fundamental law of risk and money management, as follows:

We define M as the account equity, R as the percent risk, P_i as the entry price, P_o as the exit price, and N as the number of shares or contracts. Then, equation 5.3 becomes

$$M = \frac{|P_o - P_i| \cdot N}{R} \qquad (5.9)$$

In equation 5.9, the numerator is the amount risked S, which is equal to the difference between the entry and exit price times the number of contracts or shares. The absolute value of the difference between the entry price and the exit price is taken to account for both long and short positions. Where the stop-loss is a fixed number of points, then

$$P_o = P_i \pm S_i \qquad (5.10)$$

which means that the exit price is equal to the entry price, plus or minus the stop-loss S_i in points, depending on whether the trade is long or short.

After combining equations 5.9 and 5.10 we obtain

$$M = \frac{S_i \cdot N}{R} \qquad (5.11)$$

Taking the absolute value is no longer required since S_i is by definition a positive number. After solving equation 5.11 for the number of shares N, we get the following:

$$N = \frac{M \cdot R}{S_i} \qquad (5.12)$$

Thus, we have derived the risk percent position-sizing formula where the stop-loss is in points. Next, we consider the case of a stop-loss percent as follows:

$$P_o = P_i \pm S_p \cdot P_i \qquad (5.13)$$

In this case, the exit price is equal to the entry price, plus or minus a fraction S_p of the entry price, depending on whether the trade is long or short. After combining equations 5.9 and 5.13 we obtain

$$M = \frac{S_p \cdot P_o \cdot N}{R} \qquad (5.14)$$

and we can now solve for the number of shares N to get the final formula:

$$N = \frac{M \cdot R}{S_p \cdot P_o} \qquad (5.15)$$

In this case, the position size depends on the entry price P_o. The price to open a position is not always known, because that depends on the order type. If unknown, an approximate entry price can be used without impacting the calculation greatly. For instance, many trading systems generate entry signals on the open of the next day and the orders are entered as *MOO* (market on open). In that case, the opening price is not known in advance but the last closing price can be used without a significant impact on the calculated number of shares N.

The number of shares calculated using the formulas just derived should always be checked against the maximum number of shares allowed based on available capital, and the minimum of the two numbers should be used. In the case of equities, the maximum number of shares allowed is simply equal to the available capital divided by the entry price. In the case of futures and forex, the maximum number of contracts allowed equals the available capital divided by the margin requirement per contract bought long or sold short.

MARTINGALE VERSUS ANTI-MARTINGALE BETTING STRATEGIES

The risk percent position method presented in the previous section is considered simple, yet it is known to be very effective. It is evident from equation 5.9 that as the account equity increases due to accumulated trading profits, the position size N calculated by the risk percent method also increases proportionally. The reverse happens when the account equity decreases. Thus, this method, even though it is fundamentally simple, is nevertheless dynamic in nature. It is also classified as an anti-Martingale betting strategy, as opposed to a Martingale one.

Martingale betting strategies increase the bet size if the account equity drops, in an attempt to recover losses and even make a profit, provided of course there is a strategy with a winning bias. Similarly, the bet size is decreased when the equity increases, for the purpose of limiting risk exposure and securing realized profits. This type of betting strategy can be used for position sizing, but many experienced traders do not recommend it. The reason that Martingale betting systems fail and often lead to disaster is that such methods guarantee in theory an eventual win if, and only if, the available equity is infinite. In reality, however, accounts have a finite size, and there are always a number of consecutive losers that, when combined with a Martingale betting method, can result in total ruin, a situation explained earlier in this chapter.

In contrast, anti-Martingale betting strategies increase the bet size while net equity increases and decrease it the other way. The risk percent position-sizing method and the Kelly formula can be classified as anti-Martingale betting systems. This type of betting system promises higher returns in exchange for a more volatile equity curve as compared to, for example, the equity curve that is obtained when using the starting trading account value instead with a fixed number of shares or contracts.

RISK AND MONEY MANAGEMENT PLAN

For beginners in the trading business, it may be prudent not to use advanced betting strategies, like the Kelly formula mentioned before, but to instead concentrate at first on trade execution and developing discipline. Thus, it may be better to use the starting trading capital value instead of the current bankroll to calculate position size using a fixed risk percent method. The transition to an anti-Martingale optimal betting strategy should be made only after there is enough data regarding system performance in actual trading.

Novice traders or experienced ones using a newly developed trading system should always keep in mind that things may not turn out the way they expect them to, and thus they should be very careful with risk and money management. The following plan is recommended:

1. Retail traders should calculate the starting trading capital requirement using the formulas developed in this chapter. This is recommended for new trading accounts less than $200,000.

2. For the first six months, calculate position size using the risk percent method with R = 1% and use the starting equity value, in the case of an equity increase, or the current bankroll, in the case of an equity drop. This will result in lower position size and reduced overall exposure to start with.

3. If the system's actual performance is within expected levels after six months of trading, and the trader has become comfortable with the system, the current bankroll can be used for calculating position size and R can be increased to 2%.

4. Keep a log of all trades and calculate the success rate, average win, average loss, and other important system performance parameters. If after the first year the performance parameters match or exceed their expected values and seem to be stable, then an optimal position method, such as the Kelly formula, can be used in place of the risk percent method. In case a transition to another position method is decided on, it is a good idea to always compare the position size and effective risk percent of the method selected to the position size of the percent risk method with R = 2%.

5. Remember that everybody in the trading business, including your broker, the exchanges, and other intermediaries, wants you to trade big size because they benefit most while you assume all the risk. Do not fall into the deadliest trap of trading and overexpose your account to risk, because there is always a drawdown waiting around the corner. After all, it is the compounding of small profits that makes one wealthy in the longer-term, not the assumption of extreme levels of risk.

EXAMPLES

Question: Find the number of shares in the case of a short-term stock trading system with a constant $0.80 stop-loss. Equity value is $80,000 and risk percent is equal to 0.02 (2%).

Solution: Since the stop-loss is in points, equation 5.11 is used as follows:

$$N = \frac{80,000 \times 0.02}{0.80} = 2,000 \, shares$$

Question: Find the number of shares for a short-term SPY trading system with a 5 percent stop-loss and risk percent equal to 1.5 percent. Equity value is $125,000 and the entry price is $127.00.

Solution: In this case, equation 5.15 is appropriate. By plugging in the numbers we get:

$$N = \frac{125,000 \times 0.015}{0.05 \times 127.00} = 295.28 \, shares$$

The result is rounded to 300 shares.

Question: Joe has decided to trade the QQQQ ETF (exchange-traded fund). His position size will always be 500 shares and the stop-loss always equal to $1. What is the minimum account equity required so that the risk percent will be always less than or equal to 2 percent?

Solution: The solution is obtained by applying equation 5.11:

$$M = \frac{\$1 \times 500}{0.02} = \$25,000$$

Thus, the minimum equity is $25,000. An amount less than that will result in a percent risk in excess of 2 percent. As an example, if the account equity drops to $10,000, then the corresponding risk percent is found by solving equation 5.10 for R:

$$R = \frac{\$1 \times 500}{\$10,000} = 0.05 \, or \, 5\%$$

The risk percent R in this case is equal to 5 percent and it is excessive as the probability of ruin increases dramatically at this level.

The previous example demonstrates the application of the fundamental law of risk and money management in determining the starting trading capital required for a given percent risk when the stop-loss is known in advance. This is especially useful in futures trading where the minimum bet size is one contract and thus the required trading capital per contract can be determined if the stop-loss amount is known in advance.

In this chapter, I discussed the benefits of prudent risk and money management and presented simple, yet very effective methods that can minimize the risk of ruin while maximizing expected returns. The quantitative approach taken here to risk and money management supplements the quantitative approach to profitability of Chapter 4; together they provide a rigid foundation for the development of systematic trading methodologies, which is the subject of the next two chapters.

PART III

Systematic Trading

Systematic trading requires, among other things, a trading system that fulfills certain performance criteria. When a model of a trading system is available, its historical performance can be evaluated and analyzed. But how does one come up with a model of a trading system in the first place?

Most trading system developers rely on experience and understanding of fundamental and/or technical analysis when searching for a set of rules, called herein a *model of a trading system*, which can be used to generate market entry and exit signals. The outcome of this complex trial-and-error process depends on the skill level of the developer. Proper analysis of the performance of a model of a trading system based on indicators, for instance, requires good knowledge of technical analysis, sufficient trading experience, expertise in software programming, and understanding of statistical analysis. It is a complex and involved process and can be successfully completed by those who possess the required skills and knowledge.

Chapter 6 outlines the process of trading system analysis and exposes some pitfalls of back testing. Chapter 7 presents an introduction to the concepts of synthesis and automation of the trading system discovery process. Analysis of trading systems is an essential part of systematic trading. The automation of analysis as part of the synthesis process of trading systems sets the stage for the development of advanced systematic trading methodologies that can offer a much needed competitive edge.

CHAPTER 6

Analysis of Trading Systems

O ne of the most popular methods for developing trading systems is to analyze the historical performance of "trading models" (*models*), which are the various building blocks that can be used to generate entry and exit signals. A trading system can incorporate several trading models, as well as additional logic and algorithms for dealing with order generation, placement, and execution. Thus, the term *trading system* is more general than the term *trading model*, because it encompasses many more functions and possibilities.

However, the trading model that is used in a trading system directly determines profitability. Consequently, it is used to analyze historical performance. Although order placement and execution methods can have an impact on profitability, these are usually considered as random effects and taken into account during analysis by adding a fixed amount to commissions paid, often referred to as *slippage*.

In this chapter, I first discuss the issue of simplicity versus complexity of trading systems. I believe this is a good start because many who develop trading systems wonder whether they should take the route of intuitive and simple rules or try to develop advanced algorithms and forecasting systems. Then, I discuss trading models, what they are and what they try to accomplish, as well as their limitations. The discussion continues with the presentation of a complete methodology for trading system development and back testing, the process I call *analysis*. The last section of this chapter deals with the pitfalls of back testing, a process that is synonymous with trading system development. I believe that the pitfalls as well as the limitations discussed throughout this chapter should be well understood before one spends time and effort in developing trading systems.

SIMPLICITY VERSUS COMPLEXITY

Systematic trading requires a model of a trading system for the purpose of generating market entry and exit signals. The model is necessary for analysis purposes and it can be used for automatic generation of signals, often with slight modifications and/or additions. The structure of the model can be as simple as a few empirical rules, technical and/or fundamental, or even a complex mathematical algorithm. However, simplicity or complexity should not be used as a criterion for evaluating the potential of a model used in systematic trading.

Some have argued against complexity without offering a rigorous definition of what constitutes a complex trading system, as opposed to a simple one, and without presenting convincing evidence to support their claims. For instance, some have argued in the literature that a model must be simple to perform in actual trading. On the opposite side, others have bragged about the complexity of their systems and the fact that they cannot be easily replicated, which is something that in their opinion offers an edge.

From a philosophical viewpoint, simplicity and complexity can be considered as two different paths. Where these paths meet is known as the *point of the optimum compromise*, or *balance*. The truth of the matter is that complexity and simplicity have opposite meanings but they are relational terms because they can be measured only in relation to something else. Nobody can define with certainty where simplicity ends and complexity starts. It is also true at the same time that the output of a process can be fairly simple as far as its interpretation goes but the mechanics of the process may be very complex. For example, prices can go up or down over the longer-term because there are only two possibilities present. But the process that determines the final outcome is very complex, as was defined in Figure 1.1 of Chapter 1, because observed final states are the result of market participants acting based on their own analysis and diverse objectives. Just by looking at the final outcome, one cannot extrapolate the exact dynamical structure of the process and determine its level of simplicity or complexity.

In relation to that, if a trading system is too simple it risks being predictable by other market participants and may generate too many false signals. If it is too complicated for the purpose of avoiding false signals, it risks missing out on profitable opportunities. Therefore, the optimum balance between simplicity and complexity appears to offer the best prospects for sustained profitability. As we shall see in the material that follows, it is the proper application of the analysis process that leads to profitability, rather than the degree of simplicity or complexity of the systems involved.

TRADING SYSTEM MODELING

The most important criterion that a model used in systematic trading must fulfill is its conformance to reality. For instance, a model that is intended to generate entry signals before massive buying in the stock market occurs does not conform to reality and cannot be implemented even though it sounds like it is based on a simple rule. This is because the intentions of market participants cannot be known in advance. The reality of markets dictates that the exact timing of price swings can be known only after their occurrence and not before. Despite that, trading system developers have attempted to devise indicators, with the intention of predicting the timing of similar events, that essentially can guarantee profitability. Although such efforts have not been successful, many still use the indicators and refer to them as *leading*. However, there is no such thing as a true leading indicator of market prices.

Furthermore, any trading system that attempts to exploit the structure of markets, a part of which is the participants and their actions, is doomed to fail. The actions of the participants cannot be known in advance, but only the impact of such actions on price and volume can be estimated in a probabilistic sense. For instance, any trading system that attempts to exploit information about insider buying or selling, commitment of traders in commodities, interest rate changes, or pending intervention by central banks in forex markets is not realistic in the framework of systematic trading. Such systems cannot be accurately analyzed or even implemented, although in theory they could be remarkably profitable.

One reason that practice differs dramatically from theory in the case of trading systems is that there are a lot of randomness and time delay in the information the models require in order to perform satisfactorily. For example, although commercials report their net positions in futures, the exact timing of their actions is unknown. Also, intervening central banks always surprise forex markets in order to minimize speculation. Therefore, the first and essential step every trader who desires to be a longer-term winner must take is to reject all methodologies that try to exploit the fundamental structure of the market. Systematic traders need to resort to models that conform to reality and are practical to implement, such as those that analyze only price and volume. The paradox is that theoretical models based on market structure dynamics are unrealistic to use in trading, and practical models that analyze price and volume are not theoretically sound. In systematic trading, the choice is made for the latter type, and the developer has to be aware of the limitations and deal with them in an attempt to maximize performance within the constraints imposed by the reality of markets.

As previously mentioned, the most important requirement a systematic trading model must fulfill is the capability of generating market entry and exit signals with a sufficiently high rate of success. The second requirement is that the method of generating these market entry and exit signals must naturally lend itself to a repeatable and stable process that can be precisely described algorithmically. In other words, it is not enough for a model merely to be able to generate entry and exit signals. The model must be such that if the exact same conditions arise in the future the output will be exactly the same. Therefore, in the context of systematic trading, a model is defined as a set of rules or a mathematical algorithm that generates market entry and exit signals. Generation of the exit signals may not necessarily occur at the same time the corresponding entry signals are generated, but a method for generating both entries and exits must be an integral part of the logic of the model.

Figure 6.1 illustrates the relation of the theoretical model of the market defined in Chapter 1 to a practical model used in systematic trading. The practical model uses price and volume as input. The theoretical model defines the market as the collection of its participants, whose actions are driven by information received from various sources, and the output is the price and volume for the instruments traded. On the other hand, practical models used in systematic trading rely for the most part on technical analysis methods. The input to the models is historical price/volume series

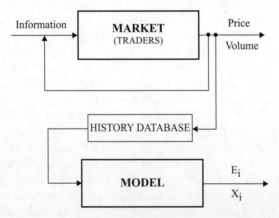

FIGURE 6.1 Relation of systematic trading models to actual market.

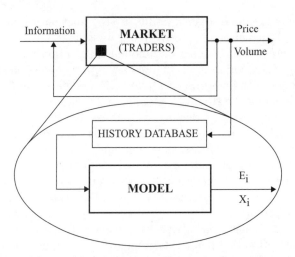

FIGURE 6.2 A model used in systematic trading as a market participant.

retrieved from a database, and the output is market entry and corresponding exit signals, E_i and X_i, as shown in Figure 6.2. An important first conclusion from the relation of a practical trading model to the theoretical model
of the market, as depicted in Figures 6.1 and 6.2, is that models used in systematic trading turn out to be market participants who react to the effects
of the actions of other participants. This can be at times a serious limitation of systematic trading and one that every trader who is relying on such
methods should be aware of.

The structure of systematic trading models raises some important
questions regarding their effectiveness. Models that generate market entry and exit signals are not exactly traditional forecasting models that attempt to simulate the behavior of markets. This is because, in addition to
their forecasting function, these models become participants of the market, which is the system for which they are used to generate a forecast. As
a counterexample, models used to forecast weather conditions do not affect the weather. In the case of models used in actual trading, the situation
is quite different. The model becomes a participant whose actions in turn
affect price direction and volume.

An important question arises at this point: Will a systematic trading
methodology perform as well in actual trading as it did during back testing? The answer is that it is possible that the actual performance will be
different. Again, the reason is that the model is part of the market during
actual trading, whereas it is not during back testing.

Back testing is a method of analyzing the performance of trading
systems, using historical data as input. Such practice became popular

because of the argument that "a trading system that performs well during back testing is a better choice over one that does not." Yet, I believe that this argument has at least one hidden assumption and an empirical shortcoming. The assumption is that history repeats itself and the reaction of the participants to the same information flow is the same. The empirical shortcoming is that the trading system is not a market participant during back testing. One way of dealing with these fundamental issues is to establish criteria that minimize the variation between historical and actual trading results. It is important to understand that the variation between actual and back-testing results cannot be brought down to zero. But since there is no other way of analyzing the performance of a trading system in advance other than by back testing it on historical data, this appears to be a natural compromise.

A naïve way of legitimizing the use of back testing is by making the additional assumption that had the trading system been used in actual trading, it would not have affected price direction. In the context of the market structure defined in Chapter 1, the implication of this assumption is that the actions of a trading system in the market do not provoke a reaction by other participants in such a way as to decrease expected profitability. The validity of such an assumption turns out to depend also on the trading time frame considered. For example, in intraday trading time frames, signals generated by a trading system are likely to provoke immediate reaction from other participants who have the ability to affect intraday price direction. However, as the trading time frame increases, the ability of market participants to affect price direction diminishes fast. The reason is that the influence of fundamental factors on price behavior prevails in medium-to-longer-term timeframes. Thus, some trading systems may exhibit the least variation between historical and actual performance in longer-term trading and the highest variation in intraday trading. But arguments claiming that back-testing results are realistic because trading systems can be assumed not to affect prices are not sound in general.

In practice, then, the variation between back-tested and actual performance can be decreased if the system is used in liquid markets. If liquidity is low, some market participants may be in a better position to move prices in order to pocket the losses of other participants. This is easier to achieve in intraday time frames than in longer-term. Thus, systematic trading can be more effective in liquid markets because it relies on a model that must maintain a minimum performance and that can be achieved only if random effects are kept minimum.

Knowing how to properly develop and apply a systematic trading methodology in speculative zero-sum games and understanding the limitations is fundamental for success. It is important to keep in mind that back testing provides no guarantee of future success but only a gross estimate of the hypothetical historical performance of a trading system.

TRADING SYSTEM DEVELOPMENT AND BACK TESTING

Back testing is an integral part of trading system development. It also goes by the names *historical testing* or *historical simulation*. The term *simulation* refers to the process of driving a model with input and observing its output. The term *back testing* can be misleading because it is not actually a process of testing the actual performance of a trading system. Instead, it provides only a simulation of the performance of a system that is likely to have been achieved had it been used in actual trading during the past. But even the use of the term *historical simulation* is not very appropriate. Simulation implies a much broader range of tests based on different types of inputs not restricted to historical data, such as a random input. At the same time, the use of the term *historical testing* can also be misleading since it could imply that the system was actually used to trade in the past. I suggest using the term *hypothetical historical performance testing* as more accurate.

In the early 1980s, when the idea of back testing trading systems had already matured, both as a concept and in terms of being practical to implement, historical simulation was an academic subject due to the high programming and execution cost involved. The high cost made it prohibitive for small fund management firms and individuals. In the late 1980s, software programs offering such capability to the retail trader were developed and the term *back testing* was invented to replace the academic term *historical simulation*, probably for marketing purposes. Simulation is a highly technical subject and sounds too complicated for the purposes of the average trader; thus the term *back testing* survived in its place. This historical account of the term is important to mention because many traders overestimate the potential of back testing. The three terms, often used interchangeably—*back testing, historical testing*, and *historical simulation*—are all acceptable provided it is understood that the results obtained are purely hypothetical.

Figure 6.3 shows a block diagram of how the process of back testing is used in trading system development. The model is driven with historical data input and the output is a set of market entry (E_i) and corresponding exit (X_i) signals. The output in conjunction with the input is used to calculate a set of performance parameters that are in turn analyzed to decide

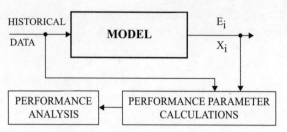

FIGURE 6.3 The process of trading system back testing.

whether the model should be used in a trading system and employed in actual trading.

Table 6.1 provides a list of some of the most important parameters calculated during back testing. Recall that in Chapter 4, and in the course of the derivation of the profitability rule, a few mathematical expressions relating some of the parameters shown in Table 6.1 were derived, and these are shown in the set of equations 6.1.

$$P = \frac{N_W}{N} = \frac{N - N_L}{N}$$

$$P_f = \frac{\sum W}{\sum L}$$

$$\overline{W} = \frac{\sum W}{N_W}$$

$$\overline{L} = \frac{\sum L}{N_L} \qquad\qquad (6.1)$$

$$R_{WL} = \frac{\overline{W}}{\overline{L}}$$

$$P = \frac{P_f}{P_f + R_{WL}}$$

Back testing is perhaps the most important step in a complete methodology for trading system development. The methodology involves implementing a model in a computer language and simulating its historical performance. It also involves the validation and analysis of the results. The steps of the complete methodology are illustrated in the block diagram shown in Figure 6.4.

Step 1: Model search. Searching for models of trading systems using traditional methodologies is a tedious, trial-and-error-process. There

TABLE 6.1 A Partial List of Parameters Calculated During Back Testing

Parameter	Symbol	Value
Profitability	P	Real: 0–1
Total Trades	N	Integer: 0–N
Number of winning trades	N_W	Integer: 0–N
Number of losing trades	N_L	Integer: 0–N
Sum of winning trades	ΣW	Real
Sum of losing trades	ΣL	Real
Profit factor	P_f	Real
Average winning trade	avgW	Real
Average losing trade	avgL	Real
Ratio of avg. win to avg. loss	R_{WL}	Real
Maximum consecutive losers	C_L	Integer: 0–N
Maximum consecutive winners	C_W	Integer: 0–N
Average bars in winners	B_W	Integer
Average bars in losers	B_L	Integer
Maximum open drawdown	D_O	Real
Maximum equity drawdown	D_R	Real

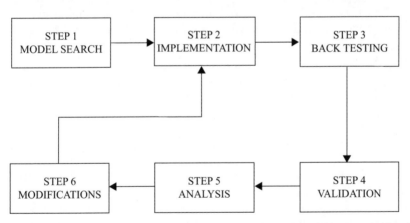

FIGURE 6.4 Block diagram of a complete methodology for trading system development.

are no recipes for success and every trader is alone in this highly demanding task. For example, some traders rely on visual inspection of charts and attempt to identify pattern formations that can be modeled as a set of simple rules. Others adopt the algorithmic route and attempt to forecast future price direction using indicators or other mathematical techniques. Thus, the complexity of models can vary widely. Many trading system developers use prepackaged systems and indicators available in software programs used for back testing. However, it is highly unlikely that a combination, or even a variation, of known formulas, indicators, or pattern formations can result in a trading system with profit-making potential. It is often the case that trading rules based on experience or on the visual inspection of price charts can offer more potential than indicators or other fancy mathematical forecasting models.

Searching for a model is a time-consuming step and can be frustrating at times. In Chapter 7, a methodology that removes the human element from this step is presented, based on the concept of synthesis of trading system.

Step 2: Implementation. After a model of a trading system is available, the next step is to implement it and back test it. In the context of the methodology discussed, it is not enough merely to discover a trading system model that one might be able to use in actual trading. It is also essential that the model logic is in a form suitable for coding in a programming language. High-level programming languages designed for this particular purpose, and offered with popular back-testing software packages, significantly reduce the time and effort required for developing and debugging programming code. Still, some trading system developers prefer to write their own code due to the limitations in the functionality of high-level-language programming.

Step 3: Back testing. Back testing involves driving the model of a trading system with historical data input and generating market entry and exit signals. The entry and exit signals in conjunction with the input are then used to calculate a set of performance parameters, including those listed in Table 6.1. Most software programs with built-in back-testing functionality also offer advanced graphics capability for plotting entry and exit points on a chart and displaying the equity curve. The use of high-level programming languages provides virtually unlimited flexibility for coding and calculating custom performance parameters and running advanced analysis to determine the statistical significance of the results.

All the computational power and implementation flexibility available nowadays is useless unless one can find a model of a trading system that will provide the much-needed competitive advantage. As mentioned previously, back testing is the process of determining and analyzing the hypothetical historical performance of a trading system; it does not guarantee future performance. In Chapter 7, the method of *synthesis* is introduced, in which back testing continues to play an important role as part of an automated process for the discovery and analysis of trading systems.

Step 4: Validation. It is highly recommended to always validate that the results obtained from back testing correspond to the intended operation of a trading system. The validation step does not try to address the limitations and pitfalls of back testing, but attempts to identify programming and implementation errors.

Specifically, validation involves the manual inspection of the back-testing results in order to determine whether the hypothetical historical operation corresponds to the intended operation. Quite often, trading system developers skip the validation step because it involves some tedious manual checking of entry and exit points and a considerable amount of calculations.

A random sample of entry and exit points followed by manual calculations based on the mathematical formulation of the model usually suffices to determine with high probability whether the implementation is correct. However, such a method of validation cannot assure that all entry and exit signals the model should have generated were actually generated. The typical reaction of back-testing software program developers is that missed signals do not matter as long as the trader follows the generated signals based on which the historical performance was calculated. However, this is a naïve response. Conditions may develop in the future that can trigger entry and exit signals, resulting in a degradation of performance. An example of missed signals will be provided in the next section of this chapter.

Step 5: Analysis. The objective of this step is to determine the suitability of a system in actual trading based on hypothetical historical performance results. Analysis is more of an art than a science, and its effectiveness depends on many factors, including skill and experience. Moreover, the results of back testing can be analyzed only in the context of the model's intended operation. Thus, the decision of whether to accept or reject a trading system depends on the results obtained but also on the trader's objectives.

For instance, if a trading system designed for use in short-term trading ends up being a longer-term trend-following system, it should be rejected even though the analysis of the results indicates acceptable performance. Many trading systems developers analyze results in absolute terms and not in relation to intended operation. This can result in a conflict between the objectives of the trader and the operation of the trading system. Therefore, the analysis of results should also include determining whether the actual operation of the system conforms to the intended operation in the trading time frame applicable. As an example, some trading system developers use ad-hoc methods to force a system to operate in the trading time frame of interest. This includes, among other things, placing a time limit on open positions. Such practice often results in gradual actual performance degradation due to random factors that can cause, among other things, future volatility to vary significantly from that of historical prices used in back testing.

In the case of back-testing results obtained for trend-following systems, the most important parameter to consider is the profit factor P_f. A large profit factor indicates that the trend-following system achieves its objective by minimizing losses during sideways-moving markets and maximizing profits during trending markets. The profitability P is of secondary importance in this case, but for reasons already explained in Chapter 4, high values may be needed to avoid degradation of actual performance due to future market conditions. On the other hand, in short-term and intraday trading systems, it is quite hard to obtain a large profit factor. In these trading time frames, the value of the profitability P in conjunction with the average win to average loss ratio R_{WL} are the important parameters to consider, although a large profit factor is always welcome.

Similar considerations apply to the analysis of drawdown levels. Trend-following systems must be able to sustain larger drawdowns, but that should not be the case with intraday and short-term trading systems, where increased values probably indicate an unacceptable streak of consecutive losers. Since the maximum number of consecutive losers that can occur in the future is a random variable, as already mentioned in Chapter 5, it is desirable that the number obtained from back testing is as low as possible.

Rejecting a trading system because of unacceptable back-testing results is much easier than rejecting a system that seems to be acceptable, but chances are it will fail in actual trading. As mentioned previously, analysis of back-testing results is a fairly complex process and its effectiveness ultimately depends on skill and experience. Eliminating subjectivity from the analysis process is as important as developing mechanical systems for the purpose of eliminating emotions from the trading process. If a trading system is accepted but the analysis was not performed properly, although emotions are eliminated from the trading operation, performance is already compromised and the benefits of systematic trading may not be realized. This is one reason it may be preferable to make the analysis of back-testing results automatic; this naturally leads to the concept of synthesis of trading systems, which will be introduced in Chapter 7.

Step 6: Modifications. After the results of a back test are properly analyzed, the trading system developer may attempt to improve performance by making appropriate changes to the model. For instance, different position exit schemes and money management methods can be implemented in an attempt to determine the best one for the particular market and intended operation. It is important to understand that the model modification step should not be confused with performance optimization. While the former is a useful practice, the latter is not.

It is very hard to establish rules for determining when a specific change made to a model transforms it into a completely different model. The only way this can be deduced is by analyzing back-testing results. For example, changing the exit logic from a profit target based on a fixed percentage of the entry price to a trailing stop may result in an increase in the profit factor while at the same time turning a short-term trading system into a trend follower. Thus, all changes made must remain within the domain of intended operation. This is a rule not always followed by trading system developers, who often analyze the results in absolute terms and ignore whether any changes made to the model transform it into a different model not conforming to initial specifications, including trading time frame considerations, initial trading capital requirements, and risk/reward parameters. If one is not careful, such practices may cause trader–system incompatibility, which can be the source of significant losses.

Optimization and implementation of ad-hoc methods to reduce losing trades must be avoided in this step. An important empirical rule is that any changes made to a model that reduce the number of losing trades without a proportional increase in the number of winning should be viewed with great suspicion. The reason for this lies in the possibility that such improvement may be just a filter of losing trades based on a limited set of conditions that just happened to be present in the historical data. When the system is employed in actual trading, new conditions may emerge not subject to the same filtering used and performance can degrade to the point of reversing from profitable to unprofitable. This can happen when the system was tested on market data spanning the period of a major prolonged trend.

For example, if the developer changes the system logic to filter out short trades by eliminating signals that occur while the difference between a fast and a slower simple moving average is positive, the number of losing trades may be reduced significantly. However, in actual trading conditions, the trend may reverse to a prolonged downturn and the system may end up filtering out short trades occurring near the peak of short-term reversals (those offering the best potential of profit in a downtrend).

By the way, this appears to be a serious limitation of many systems designed for trading equities using data from the period of the longest stock market rally in recent history, from 1993 to early 2000. As a matter of fact, traders who used black-box trading systems based on such naïve design methodology after 2000 ended up losing money.

The best way of avoiding indirect optimization due to special conditions reflected in the historical data is by selecting markets that exhibit several cycles of upturns followed by downturns, such as commodities and currencies. This is especially useful for short-term and longer-term system developing. In the case of intraday systems that do not use other time frames to filter out trades, the effectiveness of such methods to reduce the number of losers may be higher.

Model modification is another step in the trading system development process that is plagued with subjectivity and errors and will also be eliminated by the synthesis method presented in Chapter 7.

PITFALLS OF BACK TESTING

Back testing has several inherent limitations, on both a theoretical and practical level. As discussed earlier in this chapter, one severe theoretical limitation arises from the fact that when a trading system is back tested it is not a real market participant, and thus its effect on market prices is not reflected in the results. The influence of this limitation on actual performance should not be underestimated. A trading system with excellent back-testing performance can exhibit unacceptable actual performance because its operation in a specific market contributes to the development of market conditions not accounted for during back testing. As suggested earlier, systematic trading methodologies are more applicable in liquid markets, where proper adjustment of position size and risk is still necessary in order to avoid adverse effects on performance due to the reaction of other market participants. This applies especially to intraday trading systems, where actual results can vary significantly from those obtained during back testing.

Limitations of Software Programs

Even if one discounts the theoretical limitations of back testing, there are practical limitations in its implementation. Wide variations between expected and calculated results can arise due to assumptions made by the program used. This concerns mainly the validation step in the trading system development methodology illustrated in Figure 6.4.

For example, a serious limitation is skipping entry signals generated at the close of a bar on which a position of the same type (long or short) has already been closed. Similarly, it is skipping entry signals for the open of the next bar if an open position of the same type (long or short) was closed on the last bar. In technical analysis jargon, such limitation causes skipping *continuation signals* on the same or following bar where an open position is closed. Regardless of whether continuation signals turn out to be profitable, skipping them defeats the very purpose of back testing, which is the calculation of hypothetical historical performance in the most accurate way possible. Furthermore, many trading systems rely heavily on profitable trades from continuation signals because the primary force behind their signal generation is price momentum. Needless to say, a large class of trading systems designed to take advantage of continuation signals would risk rejection in the presence of such limitation in the back-testing process.

The purpose of the example that follows is twofold: First is to illustrate the philosophy of back testing to those who are not familiar with it; second is to show the importance of accurate and complete testing in obtaining realistic results. Consider a very simple system that generates a long entry signal when the close of a bar is greater than the close of the previous bar. The position is established at the open of the next bar and exited at the close. This is a simple trading system model for illustration purposes only, and its logic is given here:

Entry logic:

> If the Close (current bar) > Close (previous bar) then
> Buy on the Open (next bar)

Exit logic:

> If Open Position then exit at the Close (this bar)

Next, we perform a manual back test for the simple system just described using the price history shown in Figure 6.5. In this example, the back test is done by visual inspection and we will determine only whether there is a profit or loss for each trade generated. The price bars shown on the chart in Figure 6.5 are labeled starting with 0 for the last bar.

Manual back testing:

6: At the close of bar (6): no signal

5: At the close of bar (5): long signal since close (bar 5) > close (bar 6)

4: At the open of bar (4): establish long position

4: At the close of bar (4): exit long position (profit)

4: At the close of bar (4): long signal since close (bar 4) > close (bar 5)

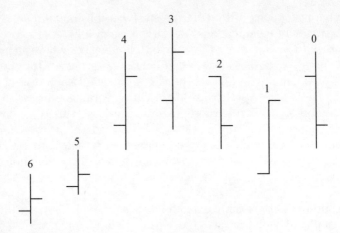

FIGURE 6.5 Hypothetical historical chart used in back-testing example.

3: At the open of bar (3): establish long position

3: At the close of bar (3): exit long position (profit)

3: At the close of bar (3): long signal since close (bar 3) > close (bar 4)

2: At the open of bar (2): establish long position

2: At the close of bar (2): exit long position (loss)

1: At the close of bar (1): long signal since close (bar 1) > close (bar 2)

0: At the open of bar (0): establish long position

0: At the close of bar (0): exit long position (loss)

Based on the manual back testing using the price history in Figure 6.5 and the logic of the simple trading system, we have determined that two winners and two losers were generated, and this amounts to a profitability of 50 percent (100 × 2 winners/4 trades). Of course, whether the system generated a net profit or loss depends on the ratio of average win to average loss, but this is not the main concern of this particular test.

Next, we are going to repeat the back test, but we will skip continuation signals that are generated on the same bar where an open position is closed. This means that the signal generated on the open of bar 3 is skipped, because at the close of bar 4 a long position was closed. The new back-testing results are shown here:

Manual back testing with continuation signals omitted:

6: At the close of bar (6): no signal

5: At the close of bar (5): long signal since close (bar 5) > close (bar 6)

4: At the open of bar (4): establish long position

4: At the close of bar (4): exit long position (profit)

3: At the close of bar (3): long signal since close (bar 3) > close (bar 4)

2: At the open of bar (2): establish long position

2: At the close of bar (2): exit long position (loss)

1: At the close of bar (1): long signal since close (bar 1) > close (bar 2)

0: At the open of bar (0): establish long position

0: At the close of bar (0): exit long position (loss)

In this case, there are two losers, but only one winner. The corresponding profitability is 33.33 percent, and the overall result may be a loss unless the winning trade can compensate for the two losers. Thus, the profitability of the system with the continuation signal omitted is lower than when it is accounted for, although the model logic is exactly the same in both cases.

Essentially, the assumed limitation in the back-testing algorithm that caused it not to take into account continuation signals resulted in an indirect modification of the trading system logic that may not be immediately obvious to the system developer. In simple words, the developer thinks she is testing a specific system, but the results she obtains are for a different system. The simple example above demonstrated the importance of the validation step, but also the possibility of obtaining chaotic back-testing results if the programs used have limitations that affect trading system operation.

Variations Due to Historical Data

The particular type of historical data series used can result in unexpected variations of the performance parameters calculated during back testing. In stock trading systems, historical stock data are normally adjusted to account for splits. In the case of futures, historical data are often adjusted to take into account contract rollovers. The method of adjustment used in conjunction with the method of generating entry and exit signals can cause back-testing results that vary significantly from hypothetical results. Note that because adjustments are not required in forex historical data, no variation in back-tested performance from hypothetical performance can arise regardless of the model logic.

Experienced stock and futures trading system developers understand that entry and exit signals that reference absolute price levels are not suitable as part of the entry or exit logic of a model, for example, a market order to sell 100 shares of XYZ stock at $100. This is because the stock may have a split in the future and the historical data series used will be adjusted to account for that. As a result, any reference to an absolute price level in entry or exit signals can result in different signals when using adjusted data and thus different performance results.

In addition, there can be variations between back-testing results and hypothetical performance results depending on the entry and exit logic even when absolute price levels are not used. These differences are classified here as (1) point variant results and (2) variant results. Case 1 applies to performance parameters expressed in points (or in an equivalent amount of currency). The values of these parameters can vary due to splits or other adjustments made to the data, but the values of several other parameters, such as the profitability, maximum number of consecutive losers, average bars in winners, and so on, are not affected. In case 2, the values of all parameters calculated during back testing vary form hypothetical values depending on the adjustments made to the data. This is a much more serious situation to consider and deal with.

To better explain how variations between back-testing results and hypothetical results arise, consider, for example, the price history of a stock from January 1994 to December 2003 that had a 2-for-1 split on June 30, 1998. This means that in order to have a continuous historical price chart, all prices before June 30, 1998, must be divided by 2, otherwise the price gap due to the split will cause distorted back-testing results. If we back test a trading system first with the actual data and then with the split-adjusted data, the two back tests will show different point values for most calculated performance parameters. Specifically, all parameters expressed in points (or equivalent amount of currency) in the case of the split-adjusted data will differ from those obtained in the case of the actual (unadjusted) data by a factor of 2 for the period before the split took place. However, the values of some parameters, such as those of profitability and of maximum consecutive losers, are in most cases not affected. This means that a back test based on the full, split-adjusted price history will produce parameters with values that do not correspond to the values that would have been obtained (hypothetically) had the system been used to trade the stock. This is what is meant by a variation between back-testing results and hypothetical results.

The worst-case scenario is where the results are unrealistic because of a reference in the model logic to price levels that do not occur in the adjusted data but would have occurred in the actual data. In this case, all calculated parameters, including profitability, number of winners and losers, net profit, drawdown, and so forth, are meaningless numbers. Similar considerations hold in the case of futures contracts since there are regular rollover dates on which adjustments must be made to the price history. As mentioned earlier, historical forex data are not subject to adjustments and the same holds for cash indexes and spot commodity prices.

TABLE 6.2 Effect of Data Adjustments on Back-Testing Results

Stops	Stock Data (Split-adjusted)	Futures Data (Continuous contracts)	Spot Forex Data
Percent	Point variant	Variant	Invariant
Variable	Point variant	Invariant	Invariant
Point	Variant	Invariant	Invariant

The effects of adjustments made to stock and futures historical data on back-testing results are summarized in Table 6.2, assuming that no references to absolute price levels are made in the entry or exit part of a trading system. It is also assumed that all entry signals are generated based on conditions derived from indicators or chart patterns. For an exit strategy, variable, percent, or point stops based on the entry price are considered. Variable stops are the result of exit signals using indicators, chart patterns, or trailing stops, and the exit price is not known when the entry occurs. Percent stops are calculated based on a percentage of the entry price after an entry signal is generated. Point stops are increments added to the entry price. In the last two cases, the exact exit price is known as soon as the entry price is known.

From Table 6.2 it may be seen that point stops in conjunction with stock split–adjusted data and percent stops in conjunction with continuous futures contracts produce variant results. *Variant* means that the back-testing results in a given time period vary from hypothetical results. In the case of stocks, as mentioned earlier, the best-case scenario is when split-adjusted data are used with percent stops, and the result is variance of all parameters expressed in points but invariance of parameters expressed as a ratio or as a simple count. In continuous futures contracts, variant results are obtained when using percent stops. This is due to the fact that in the case of futures contracts the adjustments are based on the subtraction or addition of a constant. In the case of stocks, the adjustments are based on dividing prices by a constant, and this is the reason point stops produce variant results.

To summarize, in the case of split-adjusted stock data, use of percentage or variable stops is appropriate, but the parameters calculated during back testing must be carefully analyzed because the values of some parameters expressed in points maybe over- or understated. For example, depending on the back-testing method used, net profit may be understated in the case of split-adjusted data (and overstated in reverse split-adjusted data); the same will apply for the drawdown. Thus, if a stock had several splits in its price history and the drawdown value obtained is not adjusted properly, the results can be highly misleading. In continuous futures contracts, it makes sense to use point or variable exits. In that case, the values of the parameters calculated will correspond to the hypothetical trading system performance for the time period considered in the test. As already mentioned and also shown in Table 6.2, any back-testing results using spot forex data are always invariant because no splits or other adjustments are made to such series.

Unless a trading system developer is extremely careful, back testing can easily turn into a chaotic process and any results obtained can be misleading. We have considered two factors that can influence the accuracy of back-testing results:

1. Software limitations
2. Historical data adjustments

The only way for a trading system developer to avoid the pitfalls of back testing is by validating the results of each test, indicated as step 4 in the complete methodology in Figure 6.4. One cannot know in advance how hidden software limitations and data adjustments can interfere even in the case of simple trading systems and alter their logic in an indirect way. Although software programs with back-testing capability give the impression that testing and analyzing trading systems is a relatively easy task, reality is different and the whole process can easily turn chaotic. The view that profitable trading systems can be developed by just writing a few lines of code using a high-level computer language is naïve and experienced traders know that is not the case. Learning the proper way of developing profitable trading systems while avoiding the pitfalls is a slow process whose efficiency and effectiveness increase as a function of time and experience gained from actual trading and by risking real funds under actual market conditions.

In this chapter, the process of development of trading systems via the use of analysis was discussed and the various steps followed were described. It was shown that successful analysis relies heavily on ad-hoc ways of discovering trading system models and on subjective analysis of the results obtained from back testing. I have serious doubts that the majority of trading system developments can be successful with analysis and overcome these serious shortcomings, which are the deeper cause of frequent system failures and loss of capital. As an alternative to analysis, I came up with the process of synthesis of trading systems in the early 1990s, which is described in more detail in the next chapter.

CHAPTER 7

Synthesis of Trading Systems

The most important element of a systematic trading methodology is a profitable trading system. It is not merely enough to have a high-speed Internet connection, a platform with direct order execution, fancy charts, real-time news, and analysis tools. Systematic trading requires a consistent method of generating entry and exit signals that can be implemented in a computer language, back-tested, and then, preferably, integrated with real-time data and direct execution platforms. Traders who appreciate the advantages systematic trading has to offer over conventional methodologies spend considerable time and effort developing trading systems. This involves, among other things, searching for new ideas, coding the logic of candidate trading systems, and analyzing back-testing results. All this translates into a time-consuming trial-and-error process. In order to test a new idea, a model must be implemented and back tested and the performance results must be analyzed carefully. In many cases, it turns out that the trading system has no chance of producing consistent returns in the future because the values of some key performance parameters are not acceptable. Then, one must start from scratch with a new idea until a system that produces satisfactory performance results is obtained.

A high percentage of new traders who desire to adopt a systematic approach find the trial-and-error methodology of system development frustrating. Sooner or later, after a number of unsuccessful attempts to come up with a profitable system, they give up to adopt other trading styles. Thus, the main cause of frustration is the traditional methodology of system development followed, which is fundamentally a trial-and-error process.

In addition, this methodology requires a source of new ideas in order to keep the trial-and-error process going with the hope of a final convergence to an acceptable system. But even in the presence of a source of new ideas, besides being time consuming, the process of testing and analysis has several pitfalls, as already discussed in Chapter 6.

The realities of traditional modeling, testing, and analysis used for the purpose of developing systematic trading systems can be overcome and dealt with only by a small percentage of traders who possess the skills and expertise required for accomplishing their objectives. The rest are discouraged from the start because they lack the skills and experience. Parting with a few thousand dollars to purchase user-friendly software packages for trading system development does not make things any easier. Knowledge of software programming is still a prerequisite for developing systems, even when using those user-friendly programs. Abstract ideas must be translated into a mathematical model and then into some custom high-level computer code. Thus, the requirements point to an unrealistic task for the majority of traders.

FROM ANALYSIS TO SYNTHESIS

One way of dealing with the harsh realities of the traditional process of developing trading systems is the concept of synthesis. The term *synthesis* is defined as a systematic process by means of which trading systems that fulfill user-defined performance criteria and risk/reward parameters can be discovered in a fully automated fashion.

In order to understand how such a concept might work in principle, let us first review the traditional trading system development methodology shown in Figure 7.1. According to this widely followed methodology, a model of a trading system must be identified in advance by some means. The identification process can be based on empirical rules, chart analysis, technical analysis indicators, traditional chart pattern formations, candlestick pattern formations, and so forth.

After the model is identified, it must be coded in a computer language so that its historical performance can be tested. This is known as the implementation step. Many developers use a high-level programming language for this step, which is available as part of a commercial software program specifically designed for this purpose, but others prefer to write custom code.

The back-testing step involves driving the model with historical data input to affect generation of market entry and exit signals followed by the calculation of a set of performance parameters based on the price levels at

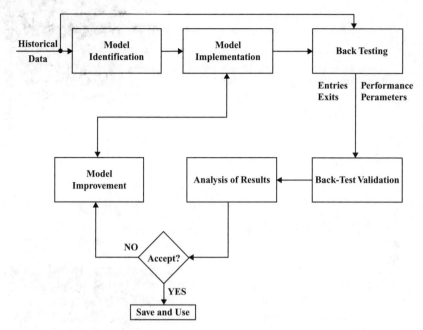

FIGURE 7.1 Traditional methodology of trading system development.

which the signals occurred. A partial list of some important performance parameters was given in Chapter 6, Table 6.1.

As soon as the back-test results are obtained, a manual validation often follows in order to verify that the trading system operates according to specifications. If the results are successfully validated, then a performance analysis is carried out to determine whether the trading system should be used in actual trading. Besides the obvious requirement that the trading system must be profitable along the time history considered in the analysis, what constitutes an acceptable performance depends on several factors and requirements that must be taken into account. For instance, if the intended operation of the system is in short-term time frames but from the back-test results it appears that it is acting like a trend-following system, then its logic must be modified to conform to the requirements set in advance. Similarly, if a system was designed for day trading use but it generates only a few trades per week, then it is probably not suitable for this task. If the trading system performance is not acceptable and modifications to the model logic must be made, the process is repeated. It is clear that this methodology of trading system development is inherently a trial-and-error process based on model identification, back testing, analysis, and modifications.

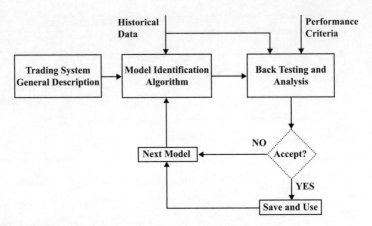

FIGURE 7.2 Methodology of synthesis of trading systems.

The methodology of synthesis of trading systems is outlined in Figure 7.2. The heart of this trading system development process is an identification algorithm. The input to the identification algorithm is the general description of the models to look for and the output is the logic of candidate models in a form that can be used to analyze historical performance. The determined logic is also used as the input to the back-testing and analysis steps along with the user-defined performance criteria. The back-testing step involves the calculation of a set of performance parameters of the identified models and the analysis step determines whether the performance criteria defined by the user are satisfied. If the performance of a candidate model is acceptable, then its logic is saved for later use in actual trading. If the performance fails to satisfy the user-defined criteria, it is rejected and the process continues with the next identified model, and it terminates when there are no more models to test.

In the next section, the steps involved in the synthesis process are described in more detail.

THE PROCESS OF SYNTHESIS

In this section, we will take a closer look at each step of the process of synthesis of trading systems outlined in Figure 7.2.

Trading System General Description

The first step in the process of synthesis is to define the general description of the models to be identified. The need for general descriptions is dictated by the fact that no process can search for abstract models whose general properties and structure are not defined in advanced. Defining the general properties and structure of the model of a trading system does not necessarily mean defining its specific logic. For instance, a general description of a trading system model could be defined as follows:

ENTRY {[RSI (x) Op1 y] Op2 [MA (a) Op3 MA (b)]}

EXIT {MA (a) Op4 MA (b)]

where Op1, Op3, and Op4 can take values from the set of algebraic operations {">," "<"} and Op2 can take values from the set of logical operations {"AND," "OR"}. Thus, in this particular example of a general description of a model of a trading system, the relative strength index (RSI) indicator and the simple moving average (MA) crossover are used to generate entry and exit signals. This means that the general structure of the models found by the synthesis process is well defined in advance but their specific logic is unknown. For instance, we do not know whether the process will decide in favor of "AND" or "OR" after combining the RSI and the MA. More importantly, we cannot know in advance what will be the values of the parameters x, y, a, and b. The algorithm theoretically could check all the combinations and determine the best model or models satisfying the general description defined in advance. This is the essence of the synthesis process and its main advantage over analysis.

Based on the general model description of the simple example above, the synthesis process may determine that the following logic satisfies the performance criteria specified by the user:

Long entry signal if: RSI(14) < 30 AND [MA(5) > MA(30)]

Long exit signal if: MA(5) < MA(30)

In the above model, Op1 and Op4 are set equal to "<," Op3 is set equal to ">," and Op2 is set equal to "AND." The algorithm chooses the values of the variables so that the system performance fulfills the criteria specified by the system developer in the best way possible. Although in some cases the determination of parameter values may imply a sort of optimization of performance using historical data, there are cases of systems where there is no need to optimize variables because there are none present—for instance, plain-vanilla price pattern formations. Therefore, optimization is not an inherent function of the synthesis process.

Model Identification Algorithm

The determination of specific model logic from general model descriptions is the task of the model identification algorithm. The input to the model identification algorithm is the general description of trading systems and historical data. The output of the algorithm is the model logic of trading systems. The historical data are used to back test candidate trading systems. Those that do not generate enough entry signals in the price history considered are rejected immediately. This speeds up the process by avoiding analysis of performance of trading systems that do not fulfill the criterion on the minimum number of trades.

It is evident that as the trading system's general descriptions become more complex, the complexity of the identification algorithm increases, too. Therefore, the key to successful synthesis is a balance between what is defined in advance as the general description and what must be identified to determine precise models. Designing a synthesis process for trading system discovery is both an art and a science. A general identification algorithm is a theoretical possibility, but practically impossible to implement. Algorithms with reduced complexity, customized for a specific class of trading systems, have the potential of providing excellent results at reasonable execution speeds.

Back Testing and Analysis

Models of trading systems identified by the algorithm in the previous step are back tested on historical data. A set of historical performance parameters is calculated for each trading system. It is important to decide in advance which parameters must be used in a filter for selecting or rejecting systems. Also, the set of parameters used in the selection process must be based on realistic criteria. For instance, profitability, profit factor, number of historical trades, and maximum consecutive losers are parameters that are useful in selecting trading systems based on historical performance, whereas parameters such the average bars in winners or losers are of secondary importance. As the number of the parameters that must be compared to user-defined criteria increases, the complexity of the synthesis process also increases. Under such conditions, identification of trading systems that satisfy user-defined criteria may be impossible or demand unrealistic computing resources. Thus, the performance criteria must be carefully selected to be relevant for the general class of trading systems targeted by the synthesis process in the trading time frames considered.

The analysis step is essential for filtering out trading systems based on a comparison of calculated performance parameters to user-defined values. Those trading systems with historical performance that matches or exceeds expectations are stored in a database. The process terminates when there are no more systems to test.

TABLE 7.1 Analysis versus Synthesis

Operation	Analysis	Synthesis
Search for models	Manual	Automatic
Model structure	General	Specific
Validation required?	Yes	No
Model improvement?	Yes	No
Performance analysis	Manual	Automatic

ANALYSIS VERSUS SYNTHESIS

Table 7.1 shows a comparison of analysis versus synthesis of trading systems.

As seen in Table 7.1, the main advantage of synthesis over analysis is gained at the expense of the generality of the model structure. For the synthesis process to be possible, computationally tractable, and efficient, the general description of trading systems must be specified in advance. The gains from automating trading system discovery come at the expense of the flexibility general analysis can offer. For most traders, this flexibility is merely theoretical and can actually turn into a disadvantage if the necessary experience and skills are not there and the pitfalls of back testing are not understood. It appears that synthesis is a much more powerful methodology than analysis in the context of systematic trading. It is only when analysis becomes an integral step of an automated process of trading system identification that subjectivity and emotions are fully removed from the trading process. Automating the signal generation and order placement is not enough to claim a level of systematic trading free of subjectivity and emotions, if the trading systems used to generate the signals were identified via a subjective and emotional process in the first place.

EXAMPLES OF TRADING SYSTEM SYNTHESIS

A good way to demonstrate the process of synthesis of trading systems is by the use of some examples. In this section, I present four examples where synthesis is used in the case of trading systems that consist of models based on price patterns. The first example uses synthesis not only to discover trading models based on price patterns but at the same time to investigate the risk/reward levels possible in a specific market. The second example deals with the synthesis of trading models based on price patterns that use a delay in placing a trade. This example demonstrates the efficiency of the synthesis process in dealing with more advanced trading strategies. The third example investigates the robustness of the trading models identified through an application of the synthesis process to a specific market. Finally, the fourth example shows the flexibility that synthesis offers in dealing with the dynamics of different time frames and in particular how short-term trading systems can be used to simulate trend following.

Example 1: Determination of Attainable Profitability Levels

This example takes advantage of the power of the synthesis process for the purpose of determining profitability levels that can be achieved in two very popular markets, the FTSE and DAX futures. In the context of the profitability rule that was discussed in Chapter 4, this is equivalent to whether low profitability systems with a high R_{WL} ratio or high profitability systems with a low R_{WL} ratio, or maybe both, are possible to identify in those markets.

The analysis concentrates on short-term trading systems based on price patterns of the following general structure:

Long entry signal:

If {long pattern logic} then

Buy tomorrow on the open with

Profit target price at Entry Price $\times (1 + T/100)$

Stop-loss price at Entry Price $\times (1 - S/100)$

Short entry signal:

If {short pattern logic} then

Sell tomorrow on the open with

Profit target price at Entry Price $\times (1 - T/100)$

Stop-loss price at Entry Price $\times (1 + S/100)$

where T and S are the profit target and stop-loss values, respectively, expressed as percentages.

The general structure of short-term trading systems based on price patterns considered in this example is complete in the sense that it includes a precise method of generating entry and exit signals. The entry signal generation is based on the conditions that define the price patterns and indicated as "long pattern logic" and "short pattern logic" in the general structure above. The exit signals are generated along with the entry signals and the position exit levels are calculated based on the entry price.

The following performance criteria will be used in the synthesis process:

Minimum number of historical trades $N > 27$

Maximum consecutive losers $C_L < 5$

Profit factor $P_f = 2$

According to equation 4.18, which was discussed in Chapter 4, the two parameters that can be varied when the profit factor P_f is a constant are the profitability P and the ratio of average winning to average losing trade R_{WL}. The percent profitability is calculated as the ratio of winning trades to total trades times 100, and R_{WL} is estimated according to equation 4.30 by the ratio T/S, where T is the profit target and S the stop-loss, while α is set equal to 1. This is in effect an approximation; the actual R_{WL} values will be calculated during back testing and they may vary from estimated values. However, the estimate is used in conjunction with equation 4.18 only for the purpose of calculating the minimum profitability P. Since the profit factor is equal to 2, there is already a safety factor in place to avoid getting systems with negative equity performance in case actual R_{WL} values turn out to be much lower than the estimated values.

The first step in the study involves determining whether the historical profitability of the identified trading systems based on price patterns is equal to or greater than the minimum profitability given by equation 4.18, for a variety of profit target and stop-loss pairs. The second step involves the applications of the performance criteria for the purpose of trading system selection. The number of trading systems that satisfy the criteria for each profitability level will provide an answer to the problem.

It is important to realize that in the course of determining what is possible to achieve in terms of profitability levels of trading systems in the particular markets considered, an added benefit of the synthesis process is the identification of the models of specific trading systems based on price patterns.

In order to proceed, one must use a method of discovering price patterns that satisfy the performance criteria. As soon as a candidate pattern is identified, the profit target/stop-loss values will be used in the back test to determine historical profitability P, number of historical trades N, and maximum number of consecutive losers C_L.

For the purposes of this study, APS Automatic Pattern Search was used. APS is a software program that automatically discovers price patterns that fulfill user-defined performance criteria and risk/reward objectives. The regular search option of the program was used (instead of the extended search option, which produces many more patterns but takes much longer to complete). Continuous, backward-adjusted, historical data from 01/04/1994 to 10/19/2004 were used in the case of FTSE index futures.

The minimum profitability, denoted as min P%, was calculated using equation 4.18, where the ratio T/S, as already mentioned, was used in place of R_{WL}. The profit factor P_f was set equal to 2. The ratio T/S was varied from 0.5 to 1.5 in increments of 0.25, as may be seen from Table 7.2. A search for price patterns was performed by APS using a set of three pairs of profit target/stop-loss values for each value of the T/S ratio.

The results of the search are summarized in Table 7.2 and indicate that more price patterns were found in the case of lower T/S values than in the case of higher values. For instance, for a T/S ratio equal to 0.50, a profit target of 2 percent, and a stop-loss of 4 percent, APS found 11 patterns that satisfied the performance criteria—4 short and 7 long. At the other extreme of the range, for a T/S ratio equal to 1.5, only two patterns were found for T = 3% and S = 2%. Thus, we may conclude that this is an indication that the number of available patterns decreases as the value of the T/S ratio increases. More importantly, it can be seen that for higher T/S values, there is a clear shortage of price patterns that satisfy the performance criteria.

TABLE 7.2 Number of Price Patterns Found for Various Values of Target/Stop Ratio for FTSE Index Futures

T/S	T%	S%	Min P%	NP	NL	NS
	2.00	4.00		11	4	7
0.50	3.00	6.00	80	9	7	2
	4.00	8.00		1	1	0
	1.50	2.00		3	1	2
0.75	3.00	4.00	73	5	3	2
	4.50	6.00		0	0	0
	2.00	2.00		3	1	2
1.00	3.00	3.00	66	2	2	0
	5.00	5.00		2	2	0
	2.50	2.00		3	2	1
1.25	3.75	3.00	62	1	1	0
	6.25	5.00		1	1	0
	2.25	1.50		0	0	0
1.50	3.00	2.00	57	2	1	1
	4.50	3		1	1	0

NP: number of price patterns, NL: number of long price patterns, NS: number of short price patterns, T: profit target, S: stop-loss, min P%: minimum required profitability.

TABLE 7.3 Number of Price Patterns Found for Various Values of Target/Stop Ratio for DAX Index Futures

T/S	T%	S%	Min P%	NP	NL	NS
0.50	2.00	4.00	80	5	3	2
	3.00	6.00		4	2	2
1.00	3.00	3.00	66	4	0	4
	5.00	5.00		3	0	3
1.50	4.50	3.00	57	1	0	1
	7.25	5.00		1	0	1

NP: number of price patterns, NL: number of long price patterns, NS: number of short price patterns, T: profit target, S: stop-loss, min P%: minimum required profitability.

The same conclusion was confirmed by the results obtained in the case of DAX futures and summarized in Table 7.3. In this case, continuous, backward-adjusted, historical data from 11/05/1997 to 10/19/2004 were used. The ratio T/S was set to vary from 0.5 to 1.5 in increments of 0.5. In this case also, the number of price patterns decreased as the ratio increased. We can thus conclude that higher profitability price patterns with low R_{WL} values are possible in the two markets considered, whereas lower profitability ones with high R_{WL} values are more difficult to find.

Therefore, the historical price behavior of the two future markets considered in this example is such that tighter stops in relation to profit targets result in a shortage of profitable trading strategies based on price patterns, although strategies with such characteristics are highly desirable. It appears that these markets demand the assumption of higher risk per trade as compared to reward and, as a consequence, demand higher profitability (success rate).

There are possible explanations for this behavior that are outside the scope of this book. Fortunately, the study indicates the presence of historically profitable trading strategies based on price patterns; otherwise, these markets would be impossible to trade short-term for a profit using such methodology.

In order to get an idea of the model logic of the price patterns used in the trading systems identified by APS, we will look at a specific example. We will also compare the estimated values of the profitability P, ratio of average winning to average losing trade R_{WL}, and profit factor P_f to the values calculated during back testing.

Figure 7.3 shows the results generated by APS Automatic Pattern Search using the parameters listed in the first row of Table 7.2. Eleven price patterns were identified—4 long and 7 short. Each line in the results

File Name	Index	Index Date	Trade on	PL	PS	Trades	CL	Type	Target	Stop	C	Last Date
FTSE.txt	12	20041015	Open	81.97	18.03	61	2	LONG	2	4	%	20041019
FTSE.txt	5	20040811	Open	89.29	10.71	28	1	LONG	2	4	%	20041019
FTSE.txt	10	20040319	Open	83.87	16.13	31	2	LONG	2	4	%	20041019
FTSE.txt	6	20040701	Open	81.58	18.42	38	1	LONG	2	4	%	20041019
FTSE.txt	1	20040903	Open	12.12	87.88	33	1	SHORT	2	4	%	20041019
FTSE.txt	6	20040414	Open	13.16	86.84	38	3	SHORT	2	4	%	20041019
FTSE.txt	6	20040604	Open	13.33	86.67	30	1	SHORT	2	4	%	20041019
FTSE.txt	10	20040712	Open	15.15	84.85	33	2	SHORT	2	4	%	20041019
FTSE.txt	3	20040712	Open	15.71	84.29	70	2	SHORT	2	4	%	20041019
FTSE.txt	3	20040604	Open	17.07	82.93	41	2	SHORT	2	4	%	20041019
FTSE.txt	5	20040922	Open	18.18	81.82	55	2	SHORT	2	4	%	20041019

Use ✓ to select or ✗ to deselect patterns   To Back-test a pattern , highlight a line and right click or press F3

Generate MetaStock Code | Generate EasyLanguage® Code | Generate Model Logic
System Tracking | ✦ Add to Database | 🔒 Close

EasyLanguage® is a registered trademark of TradeStation Technologies, Inc.
MetaStock® is a registered trademark of Equis International , a Reuters company.

FIGURE 7.3 Pattern search results for FTSE index futures.*
Source: APS Automatic Pattern Search.

*Trade on designates whether the trade entry executed on the open or close. • PL is the percent profitability of patterns suitable for long positions. In this case PS = 100 – PL. • PS is the percent profitability of patterns suitable for short positions. In this case PL = 100 – PS. • Trades is the number of trades. • CL is the number of maximum consecutive losers. • Type is either long or short. • Target shows the profit target value used in the search. • Stop shows the stop-loss value used in the search. • C indicates the type of profit target and stop-loss; "%" stands for percentages of entry price.

corresponds to a price pattern and shows the performance parameters of the particular search. PL is the profitability of long patterns and PS the profitability of short patterns. The trade entry is indicated as the open of tomorrow, the number of maximum consecutive losers is displayed under column CL, and the profit target and stop-loss parameters are shown in the corresponding columns. The Index and Index Date columns are used by APS to classify the patterns and the last date in the historical data file is also shown in the results.

The code required for back testing the first price pattern in Figure 7.3 in Metastock was generated by APS and it is shown in Figure 7.4. The price pattern logic that corresponds to this formula code is shown in Figure 7.5 as part of a trading system that has the general structure considered in this study. The back-test results are shown in Figure 7.6.

From the back-test results shown in Figure 7.6 it may be seen that the historical profitability of this price pattern is 82 percent. This figure

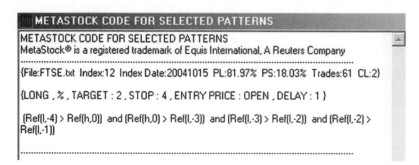

FIGURE 7.4 Metastock formula code for the first pattern in Figure 7.3.
Source: APS Automatic Pattern Search.

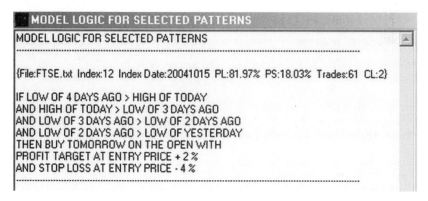

FIGURE 7.5 Pattern logic for the first pattern in Figure 7.3.
Source: APS Automatic Pattern Search.

exceeds the minimum required profitability of 80 percent, which was calculated using the profitability rule (equation 4.30 with $\alpha = 0$). The profit factor P_f is equal to 2.2, greater than the required value of 2. Finally, the ratio of average winning to average losing trade R_{WL} is 0.48, and this value is fairly close to the estimated value of 0.50 using the ratio of profit target to stop-loss T/S. Thus, the Metastock back-test results confirm the performance results obtained by the synthesis process of APS but more importantly the validity of some of the assumptions made in the study, such as using the ratio T/S in place of R_{WL}.

In this example of synthesis we considered trading systems that belong to a general class of short-term trading systems based on price patterns. Metastock formula code, Tradestation Easylanguage code, and Wealth-Lab script for selected FTSE and DAX price patterns, which were generated for the purpose of this study, are provided in the appendix of this

```
System Report (Points Only Test)  - FTSE

Item                        Value      Item                     Value
Total net profit            2991.6997  Open position value      35.5000

Current position            Long       Date position entered    10/18/2004

Total closed trades         61         Commissions paid         0.0000
Avg profit per trade        48.4623    Avg Win/Avg Loss ratio   0.48
Total long trades           61         Total short trades       0
Winning long trades         50         Winning short trades     0

Total winning trades        50         Total losing trades      11
Amount of winning trades    5420.1396  Amount of losing trades  -2463.9402
Average win                 108.4028   Average loss             -223.9946
Largest win                 232.5000   Largest loss             -370.0000
Average length of win       11.58      Average length of loss   8.18
Longest winning trade       67         Longest losing trade     18
Most consecutive wins       18         Most consecutive losses  2

System close drawdown       -261.5400  Profit/Loss index        54.84
System open drawdown        -261.5400  Reward/Risk index        91.96
Max open trade drawdown     -147.0000  Buy/Hold index           10025.24
```

FIGURE 7.6 Back-test results for the first pattern in Figure 7.3.
Source: Metastock charts courtesy of Equis International, a Reuters company.

book for those readers who do not have a copy of APS Automatic Pattern Search software.

Example 2: Determination of the Optimum Trade Input Delay

The profitability (success rate) of specific short-term price pattern formations can be increased considerably in many cases if the entry signal is delayed by a number of bars after the formation of the pattern. When used properly, a delay can act as a filter of adverse price corrections that take place immediately after a pattern is formed. The gain from using a delayed entry signal is a better entry price and that can result in some losing trades turning into winning ones. Thus, if the appropriate value of the delay is known in advance, a higher profitability may be possible over the medium to longer-term. However, although the idea of using a delayed entry appears to be an excellent remedy against short-term adverse price corrections, it also places an additional burden on the trading system development process. Before starting, a few questions must be answered:

1. When to use a delay and when not to
2. How to determine the appropriate value of the delay
3. How to identify profitable trading systems that use delayed entry signals effectively when the value of the delay is not known in advance

The answer to the first question in the case of price patterns can be given in the context of technical analysis. A delay should not be used in the case of price patterns formed during a price momentum buildup in a certain direction and that occur, for instance, near major resistance or support levels, or contribute to breakouts. In these cases, prices tend to continue moving in the direction indicated by the price pattern entry signal often without significant corrections in the short-term. However, in situations where there is decreasing uptrend or downtrend momentum and prices are not near any major support or resistance levels, some significant corrections may take place following the price pattern formation.

The reason for price corrections is fairly simple. Price patterns are caused by the actions of market participants and those early traders who cause the price patterns to form in the first place (by buying at lower levels or selling at higher levels) pocket profits immediately after the patterns are formed. Those early traders, depending on price direction, essentially satisfy the demand or absorb the supply that is generated by late traders who use the price pattern formations as signals to enter the market. The end result is corrections in prices, which in turn cause volatility to increase. Traders with tight stops often become the first victims of such corrections and wonder why, although they had a correct signal about short-term price direction, they still ended up losing. That is where a delay can play an important role by filtering out corrections in prices immediately following a price pattern formation.

The answer to the second question seems straightforward but in reality it turns out to be tricky. If a price pattern shows acceptable historical performance, one can determine fairly easily the optimum value of the delay using parameter optimization. But what about situations where in the absence of a delay a price pattern does not show acceptable performance, and it does only after the introduction of a delay? How does one identify price patterns suitable for using with a delay given zillions of unprofitable pattern formations? This is one more reason the automation of the price pattern discovery process is highly desired and that points to the synthesis process discussed earlier in this chapter.

The answer to the third question is related to that of the second in the sense that it is quite difficult to identify profitable price pattern formations visually when the value of the delay is not known. This is because just by looking at 10 bars on a chart, for instance, and without knowing the proper value of the delay to use, one cannot know which part of the formation is the pattern and which is the delay. Thus, one is normally forced to restrict the search to profitable patterns without delay that stay profitable after a delay is introduced. As we will see in the following, this reduces the number of candidate price patterns significantly unless a suitable automation of the process is available.

A Brief Introduction to Price Patterns

A Price Pattern Is a Formation of Price Bars on a Chart

The three price bars labeled 0, 1, and 2 form the price pattern shown in case A of Figure 7.7. The most recent bar in the price pattern formation is denoted as bar 0 and referred to as "today." Bar 1 is referred to as "yesterday" and bar 2 is referred to as "2 days ago," and so on.

From case A of Figure 7.7 it may be seen that the close of the last bar, or today's close, is higher than the high of bar 2, the high of 2 days ago. This relationship can be expressed mathematically as follows:

Close of today > High of 2 days ago

Using the same reasoning as above, it is also the case that

Close of 2 days ago > Open of today

The complete description of the price pattern shown in case A of Figure 7.7 can be obtained by following the same reasoning; the full set

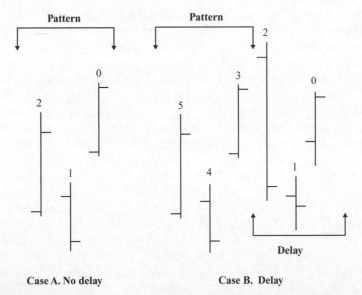

FIGURE 7.7 Case A: A 3-bar price pattern. Case B: The price pattern of case A with a 3-bar delay added.

of rules that completely define the price pattern formation beyond any ambiguity is given here:

> High of today > Close of today AND
>
> High of 2 days ago > Close of 2 days ago AND
>
> Open of today > Low of today AND
>
> Close of today > High of 2 days ago AND
>
> High of yesterday > Open of yesterday AND
>
> Low of today > High of yesterday AND
>
> Open of 2 days ago > Low of 2 days ago AND
>
> Close of yesterday > Low of yesterday AND
>
> Open of yesterday > Open of 2 days ago AND
>
> Close of 2 days ago > Open of Today AND
>
> Low of 2 days ago > Close of yesterday

This set of 11 inequalities uniquely describes the price pattern formation shown in case A of Figure 7.7. These inequalities (also referred to as the *price pattern logic*) can be combined with appropriate money management and trade entry point into a complete system for trading a specific market M in a given time frame. As an example, if the trade entry point is on the open of the day following the price pattern formation, the profit-target is T, and the stop-loss is S, both expressed as a percentage of the entry price, the trading system model structure for long/short positions can take the following form:

> **{Time frame: daily, Market: M}**
>
> **If {long pattern logic} then**
>
> Buy tomorrow on the open with
>
> Profit target price at Entry Price $\times (1 + T/100)$
>
> Stop-loss price at Entry Price $\times (1 - S/100)$
>
> **If {short pattern logic} then**
>
> Sell tomorrow on the open with
>
> Profit target price at Entry Price $\times (1 - T/100)$
>
> Stop-loss price at Entry Price $\times (1 + S/100)$

where "long pattern logic" and "short pattern logic" are inequalities connected by the Boolean operator AND, as with the set of 11 inequalities that define the pattern in case A of Figure 7.7. Using the same methodology, the logic of any price pattern formation can be incorporated into a complete trading system model and used to back test its performance or generate signals in actual trading.

Delay Patterns

The number of price bars that follow the last bar in a price pattern formation and determine when a signal is generated is the value of the "delay." Note that the bars contributing to the value of the delay do not affect the price pattern formation but merely specify how long to wait before generating a signal, long or short. The logic of the price pattern with the delay added is referred to as the *delay pattern* and can be obtained simply by adding the delay value to shift backwards each price bar in the formation. Thus, in case B of Figure 7.7, bars 3, 4, and 5 now form the price pattern and bars 2, 1, and 0 represent the delay. The signal is generated at the open of the bar following bar 0. The logic of the delay price pattern is then given as follows:

> High of 3 days ago > Close of 3 days ago AND
>
> High of 5 days ago > Close of 5 days ago AND
>
> Open of 3 days ago > Low of 3 days ago AND
>
> Close of 3 days ago > High of 5 days ago AND
>
> High of 4 days ago > Open of 4 days ago AND
>
> Low of 3 days ago > High of 4 days ago AND
>
> Open of 5 days ago > Low of 5 days ago AND
>
> Close of 4 days ago > Low of 4 days ago AND
>
> Open of 4 days ago > Open of 5 days ago AND
>
> Close of 5 days ago > Open of 3 days ago AND
>
> Low of 5 days ago > Close of 4 days ago

Alternatively, one can retain the original bar numbering in the price pattern formation, as in case A of Figure 7.7, and use an input delay count to guarantee the proper generation of the signal. The appropriate formulation of the logic of the delay pattern depends on the available functions and capabilities of the back testing or the implemented real-time trading program. For instance, in Metastock one can retain the original logic of the price pattern and specify the delay in the option settings of the Tester function. In Tradestation or Wealth-Lab, it is better to shift the bars to account for the delay.

The application of a delay can turn some losing trades into winners. But the opposite can happen as well, and some winning trades can turn into losers. Thus, any application of delayed entry signals must be done only after careful analysis and back testing.

APS Automatic Pattern Search was used to search for delay patterns in FTSE index futures data. APS is a software program that automatically discovers price patterns that fulfill user-defined performance criteria and risk/reward parameters. The regular search option of the program was used in the search (instead of the extended search option, which produces many more patterns but takes much longer to complete). Continuous, backward-adjusted, historical price data from 01/04/1994 to 10/19/2004 were used for FTSE index futures and the results for patterns without delay are shown in Figure 7.8. A total of 11 price patterns were identified by APS that satisfied the performance parameters shown in Table 7.4. Each line in the results, shown in Figure 7.8, represents a price pattern and its corresponding performance parameters.

Out of the 11 price patterns without delay shown in Figure 7.8, 4 are long patterns and the remaining 7 are short. Figure 7.9 shows the results of

File Name	Index	Index Date	Trade on	PL	PS	Trades	CL	Type	Target	Stop	C	Last Date
FTSE.txt	3	20040712	Open	15.71	84.29	70	2	SHORT	2	4	%	20041019
FTSE.txt	12	20041015	Open	81.97	18.03	61	2	LONG	2	4	%	20041019
FTSE.txt	5	20040922	Open	18.18	81.82	55	2	SHORT	2	4	%	20041019
FTSE.txt	3	20040604	Open	17.07	82.93	41	2	SHORT	2	4	%	20041019
FTSE.txt	6	20040701	Open	81.58	18.42	38	1	LONG	2	4	%	20041019
FTSE.txt	6	20040414	Open	13.16	86.84	38	3	SHORT	2	4	%	20041019
FTSE.txt	1	20040903	Open	12.12	87.88	33	1	SHORT	2	4	%	20041019
FTSE.txt	10	20040712	Open	15.15	84.85	33	2	SHORT	2	4	%	20041019
FTSE.txt	10	20040319	Open	83.87	16.13	31	2	LONG	2	4	%	20041019
FTSE.txt	6	20040604	Open	13.33	86.67	30	1	SHORT	2	4	%	20041019
FTSE.txt	5	20040811	Open	89.29	10.71	28	1	LONG	2	4	%	20041019

Results for FTSE_NO_DELAY.epr - 11 patterns found

Use ✓ to select or ✗ to deselect patterns   To Back-test a pattern, highlight a line and right click or press F3

Generate MetaStock Code | Generate EasyLanguage® Code | Generate Model Logic

System Tracking | ✦ Add to Database | Close

EasyLanguage® is a registered trademark of TradeStation Technologies, Inc.
MetaStock® is a registered trademark of Equis International, a Reuters company.

FIGURE 7.8 Search results for price patterns with no delay in FTSE index futures.*
Source: APS Automatic Pattern Search.

*Trade on designates whether the trade entry executed on the open or close. • PL is the percent profitability of patterns suitable for long positions. In this case PS = 100 − PL. • PS is the percent profitability of patterns suitable for short positions. In this case PL = 100 − PS. • Trades is the number of trades. • CL is the number of maximum consecutive losers. • Type is either long or short. • Target shows the profit target value used in the search. • Stop shows the stop-loss value used in the search. • C indicates the type of profit target and stop-loss; "%" stands for percentages of entry price.

TABLE 7.4　Parameters Used in the Search for Patterns with and without Delay

Trade Input	Open of Next Day
Profit target	2% of entry price
Stop-loss	4% of entry price
Minimum profitability	80% (min Profit factor = 2)
Minimum number of trades	28
Maximum consecutive losers	5

Results for FTSE_DELAY.epr - 32 patterns found

File Name	Index	Index Date	Trade on	PL	PS	Trades	CL	Type	Target	Stop	C	Last Date
FTSE.txt	3	20040712	Open	15.71	84.29	70	2	SHORT	2	4	%	20041019
FTSE.txt	12	20041015	Open	81.97	18.03	61	2	LONG	2	4	%	20041019
FTSE.txt	10	20040730	Open1	19.64	80.36	56	1	SHORT	2	4	%	20041019
FTSE.txt	5	20040922	Open	18.18	81.82	55	2	SHORT	2	4	%	20041019
FTSE.txt	5	20041019	Open2	15.38	84.62	52	1	SHORT	2	4	%	20041019
FTSE.txt	12	20040917	Open2	19.61	80.39	51	2	SHORT	2	4	%	20041019
FTSE.txt	3	20041007	Open3	83.67	16.33	49	2	LONG	2	4	%	20041019
FTSE.txt	12	20040930	Open3	81.40	18.60	43	3	LONG	2	4	%	20041019
FTSE.txt	12	20040728	Open2	16.28	83.72	43	1	SHORT	2	4	%	20041019
FTSE.txt	3	20040804	Open3	80.95	19.05	42	2	LONG	2	4	%	20041019

Use ✓ to select or ✗ to deselect patterns　　To Back-test a pattern , highlight a line and right click or press F3

Generate MetaStock Code　　Generate EasyLanguage® Code　　Generate Model Logic

System Tracking　　✚ Add to Database　　🔒 Close

EasyLanguage® is a registered trademark of TradeStation Technologies, Inc.
MetaStock® is a registered trademark of Equis International , a Reuters company.

FIGURE 7.9　Search results for price patterns with delay in FTSE index futures.*
Source: APS Automatic Pattern Search.

*Trade on designates whether the trade entry executed on the open or close. • PL is the percent profitability of patterns suitable for long positions. In this case PS = 100 – PL. • PS is the percent profitability of patterns suitable for short positions. In this case PL = 100 – PS. • Trades is the number of trades. • CL is the number of maximum consecutive losers. • Type is either long or short. • Target shows the profit target value used in the search. • Stop shows the stop-loss value used in the search. • C indicates the type of profit target and stop-loss; "%" stands for percentages of entry price.

the same search with the delay option activated and delay values allowed in the range of 1 to 3 bars. A total of 32 patterns were found in this case, almost three times as many as compared to the search without a delay.

The results of Figure 7.9 should not be at all surprising. The introduction of the delay increased the number of price patterns that fulfill the performance parameters in Table 7.4 as expected, by allowing more patterns

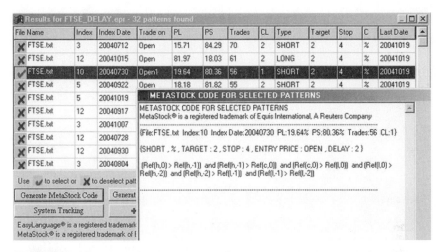

FIGURE 7.10 Metastock formula code for the highlighted pattern in Figure 7.9. *Source:* APS Automatic Pattern Search.

to turn profitable. APS determined the optimum value of the delay in the range specified. Notice that a few patterns, like the first one in the list in both Figures 7.8 and 7.9, have zero delay because the program determined that the introduction of a delay resulted in performance degradation.

As another example, let us look at the Metastock formula code for the third pattern in the list in Figure 7.9, a short price pattern with a delay equal to 1. The code generated by APS for this pattern is shown in Figure 7.10, along with information about the proper delay to apply in the Metastock Tester options. Figure 7.11 shows the back-test results generated by Metastock for the price pattern with the delay applied, and Figure 7.12 shows the back-test results for the same price pattern but with the delay set to zero.

It may be seen that the price pattern historical performance is improved when the delay is set to 1 as opposed to when it is set to 0. In addition to a lower profitability, the number of maximum consecutive losers increases to 3 from 1 in the case where there is no delay. The drawdown is also larger because some losing trades in the case with zero delay turned into winners, as was expected. More importantly, the introduction of the delay increased the profitability of the price pattern above the minimum required by the search.

The results of this study indicate that, contrary to common sense, reacting swiftly to price pattern formations may not always be the optimum short-term trading strategy. In many situations, delaying placing the trade can result in higher profitability. Of course, such methodology can be

```
System Report (Points Only Test)  - FTSE Delay
```

Item	Value	Item	Value
Total net profit	2976.2102	Open position value	N/A
Total closed trades	56	Commissions paid	0.0000
Avg profit per trade	53.1466	Avg Win/Avg Loss ratio	0.55
Total long trades	0	Total short trades	56
Winning long trades	0	Winning short trades	45
Total winning trades	45	Total losing trades	11
Amount of winning trades	5361.1299	Amount of losing trades	-2384.9202
Average win	119.1362	Average loss	-216.8109
Largest win	175.0000	Largest loss	-270.1801
Average length of win	12.69	Average length of loss	22.64
Longest winning trade	70	Longest losing trade	46
Most consecutive wins	11	Most consecutive losses	1
Total bars out	2015	Average length out	35.35
Longest out period	146		
System close drawdown	0.0000	Profit/Loss index	55.51
System open drawdown	-122.0000	Reward/Risk index	96.06
Max open trade drawdown	-269.0000	Buy/Hold index	9858.07

FIGURE 7.11 Back-testing results for the pattern code in Figure 7.10.
Source: Metastock charts courtesy of Equis International, a Reuters company.

```
System Report (Points Only Test)  - FTSE No Delay
```

Item	Value	Item	Value
Total net profit	2854.3501	Open position value	N/A
Total closed trades	54	Commissions paid	0.0000
Avg profit per trade	52.8583	Avg Win/Avg Loss ratio	0.57
Total long trades	0	Total short trades	54
Winning long trades	0	Winning short trades	43
Total winning trades	43	Total losing trades	11
Amount of winning trades	5198.3105	Amount of losing trades	-2343.9597
Average win	120.8909	Average loss	-213.0872
Largest win	210.0000	Largest loss	-267.7600
Average length of win	10.30	Average length of loss	41.36
Longest winning trade	34	Longest losing trade	161
Most consecutive wins	18	Most consecutive losses	3
Total bars out	1933	Average length out	35.15
Longest out period	143		
System close drawdown	-476.0600	Profit/Loss index	54.91
System open drawdown	-586.0600	Reward/Risk index	82.97
Max open trade drawdown	-245.0000	Buy/Hold index	9458.52

FIGURE 7.12 Back-testing results for the pattern code in Figure 7.10 with delay
set to 0.
Source: Metastock charts courtesy of Equis International, a Reuters company.

extended to other types of trading systems besides those based on price patterns, but a careful analysis must precede any application.

The logic for the first 10 FTSE index futures patterns listed in Figure 7.9 is provided in the appendix of this book. Metastock formula code, Tradestation Easylanguage, and Wealth-Lab script for each of the first 10 patterns are shown for those readers who do not have a copy of APS Automatic Pattern Search.

Example 3: Robustness of Price Patterns

This example provides an answer to the most frequently asked question about the robustness of price patterns—specifically, the question of whether price patterns that fulfill a set of performance parameters based on historical back-testing results can maintain similar performance in the future. This also relates to forward testing of trading systems for the purpose of determining their performance on out-of-sample data.

In an article published by this author (Harris, Sept. 2002) on the concept of the automatic discovery of price patterns, APS Automatic Pattern Search was used to discover price patterns for the NASDAQ-100 index tracking stock (with symbol QQQ then, which was changed later to QQQQ). The results obtained that time by APS and published in the article are shown in Figure 7.13.

Historical QQQ data from 07/11/1990 to 05/07/2002 were used in that search. A total of eight long price patterns were identified by APS Automatic Pattern Search that fulfilled the criteria in Table 7.5. Each line in the results of Figure 7.13 corresponds to a price pattern and its performance parameters as calculated by APS.

The next step in this study is to determine how the price patterns shown in Figure 7.13 performed since the time of their discovery by APS and the publication of the results. This can be achieved by back testing each pattern in the time period from 05/07/2002 to 09/28/2007. The back-testing function of APS was used for this purpose and the results for each pattern shown in Figure 7.13 are shown in Table 7.6.

It is clear from the results in Table 7.6 that all eight patterns remained profitable during the forward test period considered. This means that a trading system based on those eight price patterns for QQQ, which were developed in 2002 using a synthesis process, would have remained profitable in the following five years. Thus, the test results demonstrated the robustness of the specific QQQ price patterns.

Note that it is not necessary to analyze the results of the test for statistical significance. Obviously, the number of trades of each price pattern in the forward test is not enough to guarantee statistical significance of each individual price pattern. But when the sum of the trades of each price

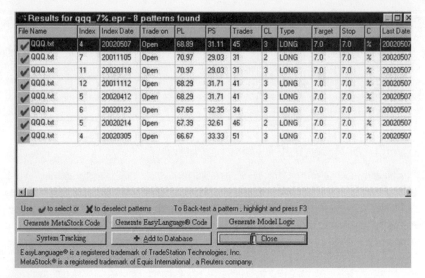

FIGURE 7.13 Search results for QQQ price patterns.*
Source: APS Automatic Pattern Search.

*Trade on designates whether the trade entry executed on the open or close. • PL is the percent profitability of patterns suitable for long positions. In this case PS = 100 – PL. • PS is the percent profitability of patterns suitable for short positions. In this case PL = 100 – PS. • Trades is the number of trades. • CL is the number of maximum consecutive losers. • Type is either long or short. • Target shows the profit target value used in the search. • Stop shows the stop-loss value used in the search. • C indicates the type of profit target and stop-loss; "%" stands for percentages of entry price.

TABLE 7.5 Parameters Used in the Search for QQQ Price Patterns

Trade Input	Open of Next Day
Delay	0
Profit target	7% of entry price
Stop-loss	7% of entry price
Minimum profitability	66%
Minimum number of trades	30
Maximum consecutive losers	Less than 4

pattern in the combined testing periods is considered, it turns out that the results are statistically significant.

Next, APS Automatic Pattern Search was used to search for price patterns that fulfill the criteria shown in Table 7.5 in the combined time period (back test plus forward test) starting on 07/11/1990 and ending on

TABLE 7.6 Back-Test Results for the Price Patterns in Figure 7.13 in the Period 05/07/2002 to 09/28/2007

Index	Index Date	P (%)	Trades	CL
4	20020507	69.23	13	2
7	20011105	75.00	8	1
11	20020118	60.00	10	2
12	20011112	66.67	12	2
5	20020412	59.94	17	2
6	20020123	64.71	17	3
5	20020214	72.22	18	2
4	20020305	53.85	13	2

P is the profitability; CL is the maximum number of consecutive losers.

09/28/2007. A total of 15 patterns were found, as shown in Figure 7.14. Some of the price patterns in this case are identical to those shown in the search results in Figure 7.13, and some new price patterns have emerged while a few of the original ones do not appear in the results because they no longer fulfill the performance criteria. Thus, although the range of the historical data used in the search was increased significantly, the number of price patterns that meet or exceed the performance criteria almost doubled. This is an important result because it shows that in this particular market, the passage of time affects neither the performance of price patterns nor the availability of profitable formations.

The code for selected QQQQ patterns listed in Figure 7.14 is provided in the appendix. Metastock formula code, Tradestation Easylanguage, and Wealth-Lab script for each of the patterns in the list is included for those readers who do not have a copy of APS Automatic Pattern Search and so cannot generate the search results and the code.

Example 4: Trend Following with Price Patterns

It is very difficult to identify a trend early in its formation. Most trends can be identified only after a significant portion of them have already formed. In addition, most popular indicators used for identifying price trends have significant time lag and are affected by volatility to the extent that their use in developing robust trend-following trading systems has been highly questioned. To make things more difficult, there is no proven method for exiting a position while on a trend. It is often the case that positions are closed either too early or too late. Early exits result in missing a significant portion of the trend and late exits contribute to significant drawdowns. Both are highly undesirable situations. However, it appears very difficult to

File Name	Index	Index Date	Trade on	PL	PS	Trades	CL	Type	Target	Stop	C	Last Date
QQQQ.txt	4	20070925	Open	67.24	32.76	58	3	LONG	7	7	%	20070928
QQQQ.txt	7	20070418	Open	74.29	25.71	35	2	LONG	7	7	%	20070928
QQQQ.txt	7	20070424	Open	73.68	26.32	38	2	LONG	7	7	%	20070928
QQQQ.txt	7	20070824	Open	71.43	28.57	35	2	LONG	7	7	%	20070928
QQQQ.txt	12	20070626	Open	71.43	28.57	35	3	LONG	7	7	%	20070928
QQQQ.txt	6	20070611	Open	70.97	29.03	31	2	LONG	7	7	%	20070928
QQQQ.txt	5	20070827	Open	69.84	30.16	63	2	LONG	7	7	%	20070928
QQQQ.txt	6	20070524	Open	69.77	30.23	43	3	LONG	7	7	%	20070928
QQQQ.txt	2	20070816	Open	69.57	30.43	46	3	LONG	7	7	%	20070928
QQQQ.txt	4	20070816	Open	69.49	30.51	59	3	LONG	7	7	%	20070928
QQQQ.txt	10	20070911	Open	69.44	30.56	36	2	LONG	7	7	%	20070928
QQQQ.txt	4	20070521	Open	67.57	32.43	37	3	LONG	7	7	%	20070928
QQQQ.txt	1	20070625	Open	67.44	32.56	43	3	LONG	7	7	%	20070928
QQQQ.txt	6	20070523	Open	66.67	33.33	63	3	LONG	7	7	%	20070928
QQQQ.txt	7	20061221	Open	66.67	33.33	39	2	LONG	7	7	%	20070928

Results for qqqq_7%.epr - 15 patterns found

Use ✔ to select or ✘ to deselect patterns   To Back-test a pattern, highlight a line and right click or press F3

Generate MetaStock Code | Generate EasyLanguage® Code | System Tracking | ✚ Add to Database
Generate Model Logic | Generate Wealth-Lab code | Generate TeleChart Code | 🔒 Close

EasyLanguage® is a registered trademark of TradeStation Technologies, Inc.
MetaStock® is a registered trademark of Equis International, a Reuters company.
Wealth-Lab is a trademark of WL Systems, Inc.
TeleChart is a registered trademark of Worden Brothers, Inc.

FIGURE 7.14 Search results for QQQQ price patterns.*
Source: APS Automatic Pattern Search.

*Trade on designates whether the trade entry executed on the open or close. • PL is the percent profitability of patterns suitable for long positions. In this case PS = 100 – PL. • PS is the percent profitability of patterns suitable for short positions. In this case PL = 100 – PS. • Trades is the number of trades. • CL is the number of maximum consecutive losers. • Type is either long or short. • Target shows the profit target value used in the search. • Stop shows the stop-loss value used in the search. • C indicates the type of profit target and stop-loss; "%" stands for percentages of entry price.

find a way to get an optimum balance between swift reaction and patience in trend trading.

In Chapter 3, in the subsection "Trading in Multiple Time Frames," a method was discussed for combining short-term and longer-term trading time frames. The method is based on using multiple price pattern formations to effectively achieve trend following. Here a specific example is presented that illustrates in more detail this very powerful methodology.

APS Automatic Pattern Search was used to search for price patterns in the price history of the stock of Microsoft Corp. (MSFT) spanning the period January 1990 to February 14, 2003 that fulfill the following performance criteria:

Profitability (% success rate) > 66%

Number of trades > 30

Consecutive losers < 4

Trade input: open of next day

Profit target/stop-loss = 7% of entry price

An APS search found five price patterns that met the above performance criteria, as shown in Figure 7.15. These patterns were in turn combined to develop a trading system. Each price pattern in Figure 7.15 served as a subsystem in the combined trading system. Figure 7.16 shows the back-testing results for the combined trading system for the price history

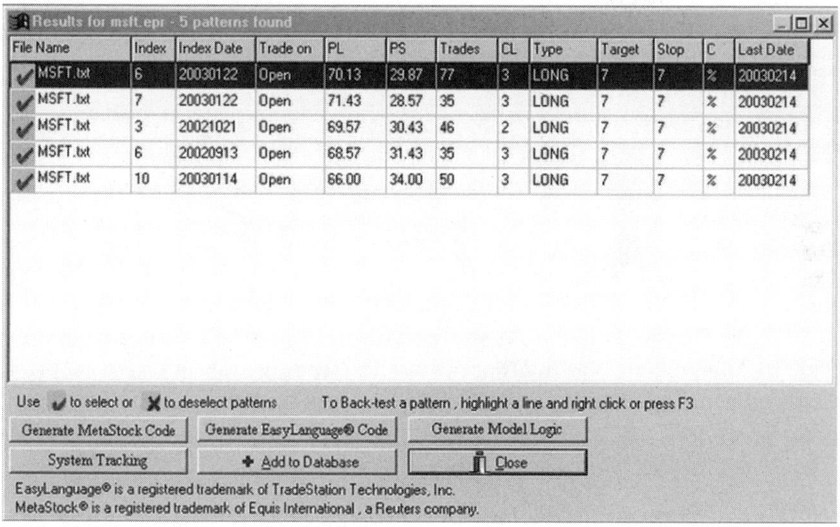

File Name	Index	Index Date	Trade on	PL	PS	Trades	CL	Type	Target	Stop	C	Last Date
MSFT.txt	6	20030122	Open	70.13	29.87	77	3	LONG	7	7	%	20030214
MSFT.txt	7	20030122	Open	71.43	28.57	35	3	LONG	7	7	%	20030214
MSFT.txt	3	20021021	Open	69.57	30.43	46	2	LONG	7	7	%	20030214
MSFT.txt	6	20020913	Open	68.57	31.43	35	3	LONG	7	7	%	20030214
MSFT.txt	10	20030114	Open	66.00	34.00	50	3	LONG	7	7	%	20030214

Use ✔ to select or ✘ to deselect patterns   To Back-test a pattern , highlight a line and right click or press F3

Generate MetaStock Code   Generate EasyLanguage® Code   Generate Model Logic

System Tracking   ✚ Add to Database   🔒 Close

EasyLanguage® is a registered trademark of TradeStation Technologies, Inc.
MetaStock® is a registered trademark of Equis International , a Reuters company.

FIGURE 7.15 Search results for MSFT price patterns.*
Source: APS Automatic Pattern Search.

*Trade on designates whether the trade entry executed on the open or close. • PL is the percent profitability of patterns suitable for long positions. In this case PS = 100 – PL. • PS is the percent profitability of patterns suitable for short positions. In this case PL = 100 – PS. • Trades is the number of trades. • CL is the number of maximum consecutive losers. • Type is either long or short. • Target shows the profit target value used in the search. • Stop shows the stop-loss value used in the search. • C indicates the type of profit target and stop-loss; "%" stands for percentages of entry price.

System Report (Points Only Test) - MSFT 01/02/1990 - 02/14/2003

Item	Value	Item	Value
Total net profit	52.6078	Open position value	N/A
Current position	Out	Date position entered	1/29/2003
Buy/Hold profit	46.4600	Days in test	4602
Total closed trades	137	Commissions paid	0.0000
Avg profit per trade	0.3840	Avg Win/Avg Loss ratio	0.73
Total long trades	137	Total short trades	0
Winning long trades	89	Winning short trades	0
Total winning trades	89	Total losing trades	48
Amount of winning trades	205.1828	Amount of losing trades	-152.5750
Average win	2.3054	Average loss	-3.1786
Largest win	7.0700	Largest loss	-7.7791
Average length of win	10.66	Average length of loss	10.46
Longest winning trade	71	Longest losing trade	62
Most consecutive wins	7	Most consecutive losses	3
Total bars out	2002	Average length out	14.51
Longest out period	65		
System close drawdown	-0.2793	Profit/Loss index	25.64
System open drawdown	-0.2993	Reward/Risk index	99.43
Max open trade drawdown	-3.6900	Buy/Hold index	13.23

FIGURE 7.16 Back-testing results of a system using the patterns in Figure 7.15. *Source:* Metastock charts courtesy of Equis International, a Reuters company.

considered in the search. This system has profitability 65 percent, an average win to average loss ratio of 0.73, and a profit factor equal to 1.34. The number of maximum consecutive losers is equal to three.

Figure 7.17 is a chart of a short-term trend in MSFT prices from July 2002 to August 2002. During that period, the trading system based on price patterns generated three profitable long signals and managed to capture a good portion of the price move. Specifically, the net profit for those three trades was $10.26, while the buy-and-hold gain for the duration of the move was near $12.

Based on these findings, the short-term price patterns captured 86 percent of the trend and did probably much better than any traditional method for trend following. For example, it is easy to check that a 5–30 simple moving average crossover trading system, which generates a long signal when the 5-bar simple moving average crosses above the 30-bar simple moving average, would result in one losing trade during the time period considered.

Another example of trend following of the same trading system developed for MSFT is shown in Figure 7.18. In this case, the short-term price trend spanned the period from June 1999 to mid-July 1999. The trading

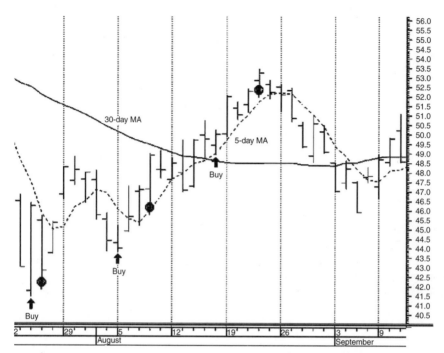

FIGURE 7.17 Short-term trend in MSFT prices from July 2002 to August 2002. *Source:* Metastock charts courtesy of Equis International, a Reuters company.

system based on short-term price patterns developed using a synthesis process generated three consecutive winning trades in that period for a net profit of $18.23 as compared to a possible maximum profit of $25 that could be theoretically achieved. That amounts to a capture of 73 percent of the short-term trend.

In must be emphasized that the trend-following ability of trading systems based on price patterns is not an inherent property but comes as an added benefit of their capability of generating multiple consecutive signals along the duration of the trend. Thus, it is an indirect but very effective way of capturing short-term, or even long-term, price moves. Figure 7.19 shows the signal generation of a trading system based on price patterns developed using a synthesis process for the SPY (spiders) exchange-traded fund over a longer-term trend during years 1994 to 1998. During that period, the system generated 18 trades and captured almost 95 percent of the buy-and-hold profit even though it was in the market only 70 percent of the time, as can be seen from the back-testing results shown in Figure 7.20. Similar systems can be developed through a synthesis process for a variety of mar-

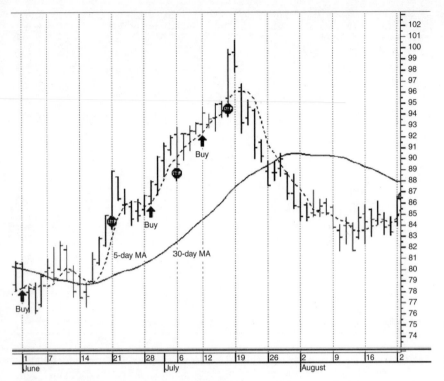

FIGURE 7.18 Short-term trend in MSFT prices from June 1999 to mid-July 1999. *Source:* Metastock charts courtesy of Equis International, a Reuters company.

kets that can generate enough profitable signals to exceed the buy-and-hold profit during longer-term trends.

AT THE END OF THE DAY ...

The markets are not mechanical generators of price and volume series where the sole task of a trader is to make the right forecast at the right time. Behind every transaction in the market there are human motives and emotions, even if transactions are electronic and trading systems are automatic. The purpose of Chapter 1 was to try to describe markets from the point of view of trading and investing. When one looks at the market as a collection of participants whose actions are driven by various sources of information, including the actions of other participants, then one can realize the limitations of back-testing and trading system analysis discussed in Chapter 6.

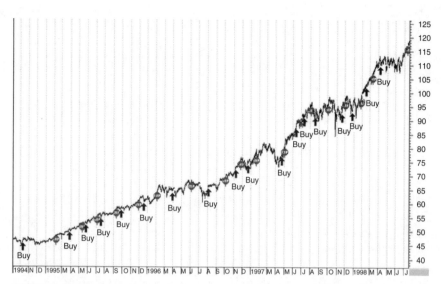

FIGURE 7.19 Price pattern signals along a longer-term trend in SPY prices.
Source: Metastock charts courtesy of Equis International, a Reuters company.

```
System Report (Points Only Test)  - SPY  1994 - 1998
```

Item	Value	Item	Value
Total net profit	68.8380	Open position value	N/A
Current position	Out	Date position entered	7/14/1998
Buy/Hold profit	72.1900	Days in test	1411
Buy/Hold pct gain/loss	N/A	Annual B/H pct gain/loss	N/A
Total closed trades	18	Commissions paid	0.0000
Avg profit per trade	3.8243	Avg Win/Avg Loss ratio	N/A
Total long trades	18	Total short trades	0
Winning long trades	18	Winning short trades	0
Total winning trades	18	Total losing trades	0
Amount of winning trades	68.8380	Amount of losing trades	0.0000
Average win	3.8243	Average loss	N/A
Largest win	5.5875	Largest loss	0.0000
Average length of win	32.67	Average length of loss	N/A
Longest winning trade	84	Longest losing trade	0
Most consecutive wins	18	Most consecutive losses	0
Total bars out	423	Average length out	22.26
Longest out period	63		
System close drawdown	0.0000	Profit/Loss index	100.00
System open drawdown	-1.0600	Reward/Risk index	98.48
Max open trade drawdown	-2.5300	Buy/Hold index	-4.64

FIGURE 7.20 Back-testing results of the system that generated the signals in Figure 7.19.
Source: Metastock charts courtesy of Equis International, a Reuters company.

Besides adopting the proper description of the market, it is also important to understand that the aim of systematic trading is wealth redistribution. Trading does not produce new wealth because it is a zero-sum game, as was discussed in Chapter 2. This implies that those planning to develop trading systems must make sure they exploit some kind of an edge, otherwise they will end up losing money. The edge may rest either on the method of analyzing trading systems and selecting the best ones to use, as was discussed in Chapter 6, or on a method of synthesis of trading systems, discussed in Chapter 7, or on a combination of these methods.

But the most important requirement for trading success is a quantitative approach to profitability and risk and money management, the topics of Chapters 4 and 5. A trader or system developer must understand the various tradeoffs imposed on the performance of trading systems and their impact on various time frames. In addition, unless proper risk and money management is applied, even the best of trading systems can turn into losers. Longer-term success depends on a fine balance between preserving capital and risking capital to harvest returns. This should be the ultimate objective of any trading method, and I hope I have provided some thoughts, techniques, and examples in this book that can contribute toward the achievement of this very difficult goal.

Codes for Selected Price Patterns

T his appendix lists the code for selected patterns from the examples in Chapter 7 that can be used with Metastock, TradeStation, or Wealth-Lab. The code is provided for educational purposes only and for studying the historical performance of the patterns. In addition, patterns can be combined in various ways to study more complicated trading systems involving advanced strategies, such as the trend-following method discussed in Example 4 of Chapter 7.

ABBREVIATIONS

Below is the list of abbreviations used in the headers of the price pattern code generated by APS Automatic Pattern Search.

PL: The percent profitability of patterns suitable for long positions. In this case PS = 100 – PL.

PS: The percent profitability of patterns suitable for short positions. In this case PL = 100 – PS.

Trades: The number of trades in the price history.

CL: The number of maximum consecutive losers.

TARGET: The profit target value.

STOP: The stop-loss value.

"%": Indicates profit target and stop-loss calculated as a percentage of the entry price.

DELAY: The entry signal delay value in bars.

Note: **Index** and **Index date** are used internally by APS Automatic Pattern Search for pattern classification purposes only.

HEADER DETAILS

Each pattern code includes a header. Here is an example that explains the meaning of the various parameters in the header:

```
{File: DAX.txt Index:11 Index Date:20050121 PL: 68.42% PS:
31.58% Trades:38 CL:3}
{LONG, %0, TARGET: 3, STOP: 3, ENTRY PRICE: OPEN, DELAY: 1}
```

Explanation: This is a long price pattern discovered in file DAX.txt with profitability 68.42%, 38 trades, and 3 maximum consecutive losers. The profit target is 3% of the entry price and the stop-loss 3% of the entry price. Positions are placed on the open of the bar following the pattern formation completion. The delay value is 1.

You can type the code of the price patterns in Metastock, TradeStation, or Wealth-Lab. If TradeStation is used, the value of the input variables (profit target and stop-loss) must be specified. The same applies in the case of Metastock where, in addition, the value of the delay must be also specified in the tester options.

QQQQ Patterns

1. Metastock Formula Code   Metastock code for selected QQQQ patterns. Metastock® is a registered trademark of Equis International, a Reuters company.

```
{File:QQQQ.txt Index:1 Index Date:20050218 PL:67.57% PS:
32.43% Trades:37 CL:3}
{LONG, %, TARGET: 7, STOP: 7, ENTRY PRICE: OPEN, DELAY: 1}
(Ref (h,-1) > Ref (o,-1)) AND (Ref (o,-1) > Ref (h,0)) AND
(Ref (h,0) > Ref (o,0)) AND (Ref (o,0) > Ref (c,-1)) AND
(Ref (c,-1) > Ref (l,-1)) AND (Ref (l,-1) > Ref (c,0)) AND
(Ref (c,0) > Ref (l,0))
```

{File:QQQQ.txt Index:11 Index Date:20041012 PL:71.43% PS:
28.57% Trades:35 CL:3}
{LONG, %, TARGET: 7, STOP: 7, ENTRY PRICE: OPEN, DELAY: 1}
(Ref (l,-3) > Ref (h,0)) AND (Ref (h,0) > Ref (l,-1)) AND
(Ref (l,-1) > Ref (l,-2))

{File:QQQQ.txt Index:7 Index Date:20041101 PL:70.97% PS:
29.03% Trades:31 CL:2}
{LONG, %, TARGET: 7, STOP: 7, ENTRY PRICE: OPEN, DELAY: 1}
(Ref (c,0) > Ref (c,-2)) AND (Ref (c,-2) > Ref (c,-1)) AND
(Ref (c,-1) > Ref (c,-3)) AND (Ref (c,-3) > Ref (c,-4)) AND
(Ref (c,-4) > Ref (c,-5))

{File:QQQQ.txt Index:7 Index Date:20041001 PL:70.59% PS:
29.41% Trades:34 CL:2}
{LONG, %, TARGET: 7, STOP: 7, ENTRY PRICE: OPEN, DELAY: 1}
(Ref (c,0) > Ref (c,-1)) AND (Ref (c,-1) > Ref (c,-2)) AND
(Ref (c,-2) > Ref (c,-5)) AND (Ref (c,-5) > Ref (c,-3)) AND
(Ref (c,-3) > Ref (c,-4))

{File:QQQQ.txt Index:5 Index Date:20050207 PL:69.09% PS:
30.91% Trades:55 CL:2}
{LONG, %, TARGET: 7, STOP: 7, ENTRY PRICE: OPEN, DELAY: 1}
(Ref (c,-1) > Ref (c,0)) AND (Ref (c,0) > Ref (c,-3)) AND
(Ref (c,-3) > Ref (c,-2))

{File:QQQQ.txt Index:6 Index Date:20050120 PL:68.57% PS:
31.43% Trades:35 CL:3}
{LONG, %, TARGET: 7, STOP: 7, ENTRY PRICE: OPEN, DELAY: 1}
(Ref (c,-2) > Ref (c,-3)) AND (Ref (c,-3) > Ref (c,-1)) AND
(Ref (c,-1) > Ref (c,-4)) AND (Ref (c,-4) > Ref (c,0))

{File:QQQQ.txt Index:2 Index Date:20050218 PL:68.57% PS:
31.43% Trades:35 CL:3}
{LONG, %, TARGET: 7, STOP: 7, ENTRY PRICE: OPEN, DELAY: 1}
(Ref (h,-2) > Ref (h,-1)) AND (Ref (h,-1) > Ref (c,-2)) AND
(Ref (c,-2) > Ref (l,-2)) AND (Ref (l,-2) > Ref (h,0)) AND
(Ref (h,0) > Ref (c,-1)) AND (Ref (c,-1) > Ref (l,-1)) AND
(Ref (l,-1) > Ref (c,0)) AND (Ref (c,0) > Ref (l,0))

{File:QQQQ.txt Index:4 Index Date:20040430 PL:68.52% PS:
31.48% Trades:54 CL:3}
{LONG, %, TARGET: 7, STOP: 7, ENTRY PRICE: OPEN, DELAY: 1}
(Ref (h,-3) > Ref (h,-2)) AND (Ref (h,-2) > Ref (l,-3)) AND
(Ref (l,-3) > Ref (h,-1)) AND (Ref (h,-1) > Ref (l,-2)) AND
(Ref (l,-2) > Ref (h,0)) AND (Ref (h,0) > Ref (l,-1)) AND
(Ref (l,-1) > Ref (l,0))

```
{File:QQQQ.txt Index:12 Index Date:20041111 PL:68.09% PS:
31.91% Trades:47 CL:3}
{LONG, %, TARGET: 7, STOP: 7, ENTRY PRICE: OPEN, DELAY: 1}
(Ref (h,0) > Ref (l,-3)) AND (Ref (l,-3) > Ref (l,-2)) AND
(Ref (l,-2) > Ref (l,-1)) AND (Ref (l,-1) > Ref (l,-4))


{File:QQQQ.txt Index:4 Index Date:20041203 PL:67.27% PS:
32.73% Trades:55 CL:3}
{LONG, %, TARGET: 7, STOP: 7, ENTRY PRICE: OPEN, DELAY: 1}
(Ref (h,0) > Ref (h,-1)) AND (Ref (h,-1) > Ref (l,0)) AND
(Ref (l,0) > Ref (h,-2)) AND (Ref (h,-2) > Ref (l,-1)) AND
(Ref (l,-1) > Ref (h,-3)) AND (Ref (h,-3) > Ref (l,-2)) AND
(Ref (l,-2) > Ref (l,-3))
```

2. EasyLanguage Code   EasyLanguage® code for selected QQQQ patterns. EasyLanguage® is a registered trademark of TradeStation Technologies, Inc.

```
{File:QQQQ.txt Index:1 Index Date:20050218 PL:67.57% PS:
32.43% Trades:37 CL:3}
{LONG, %, TARGET: 7, STOP: 7, ENTRY PRICE: OPEN, DELAY: 0}
input: ptarget (7), stopl (7);
variables: profitprice (0), stopprice (0);
if h[1] > o[1] AND o[1] > h[0] AND h[0] > o[0] AND o[0] >
c[1] AND c[1] > l[1] AND l[1] > c[0] AND c[0] > l[0] then
begin
Buy Next Bar at open;
if Marketposition = 0 then begin
profitprice = O of tomorrow * (1+ptarget/100);
stopprice = O of tomorrow * (1-stopl/100);
sell next bar at profitprice limit;
sell next bar at stopprice stop;
end;
end;
if marketposition= 1 then begin
profitprice= entryprice * (1 + ptarget/100);
stopprice= entryprice * (1 - stopl/100);
sell next bar at profitprice limit;
sell next bar at stopprice stop;
end;


{File:QQQQ.txt Index:11 Index Date:20041012 PL:71.43% PS:
28.57% Trades:35 CL:3}
{LONG, %, TARGET: 7, STOP: 7, ENTRY PRICE: OPEN, DELAY: 0}
input: ptarget (7), stopl (7);
variables: profitprice (0), stopprice (0);
```

```
if l[3] > h[0] AND h[0] > l[1] AND l[1] > l[2] then begin
Buy Next Bar at open;
if Marketposition = 0 then begin
profitprice = O of tomorrow * (1+ptarget/100);
stopprice = O of tomorrow * (1-stopl/100);
sell next bar at profitprice limit;
sell next bar at stopprice stop;
end;
end;
if marketposition= 1 then begin
profitprice= entryprice * (1 + ptarget/100);
stopprice= entryprice * (1 - stopl/100);
sell next bar at profitprice limit;
sell next bar at stopprice stop;
end;

{File:QQQQ.txt Index:7 Index Date:20041101 PL:70.97% PS:
29.03% Trades:31 CL:2}
{LONG, %, TARGET: 7, STOP: 7, ENTRY PRICE: OPEN, DELAY: 0}
input: ptarget (7), stopl (7);
variables: profitprice (0), stopprice (0);
if c[0] > c[2] AND c[2] > c[1] AND c[1] > c[3] AND c[3] >
c[4] AND c[4] > c[5] then begin
Buy Next Bar at open;
if Marketposition = 0 then begin
profitprice = O of tomorrow * (1+ptarget/100);
stopprice = O of tomorrow * (1-stopl/100);
sell next bar at profitprice limit;
sell next bar at stopprice stop;
end;
end;
if marketposition= 1 then begin
profitprice= entryprice * (1 + ptarget/100);
stopprice= entryprice * (1 - stopl/100);
sell next bar at profitprice limit;
sell next bar at stopprice stop;
end;

{File:QQQQ.txt Index:7 Index Date:20041001 PL:70.59% PS:
29.41% Trades:34 CL:2}
{LONG, %, TARGET: 7, STOP: 7, ENTRY PRICE: OPEN, DELAY: 0}
input: ptarget (7), stopl (7);
variables: profitprice (0), stopprice (0);
if c[0] > c[1] AND c[1] > c[2] AND c[2] > c[5] AND c[5] >
c[3] AND c[3] > c[4] then begin
Buy Next Bar at open;
if Marketposition = 0 then begin
```

```
profitprice = O of tomorrow * (1+ptarget/100);
stopprice = O of tomorrow * (1-stopl/100);
sell next bar at profitprice limit;
sell next bar at stopprice stop;
end;
end;
if marketposition= 1 then begin
profitprice= entryprice * (1 + ptarget/100);
stopprice= entryprice * (1 - stopl/100);
sell next bar at profitprice limit;
sell next bar at stopprice stop;
end;

{File:QQQQ.txt Index:5 Index Date:20050207 PL:69.09% PS:
30.91% Trades:55 CL:2}
{LONG, %, TARGET: 7, STOP: 7, ENTRY PRICE: OPEN, DELAY: 0}
input: ptarget (7), stopl (7);
variables: profitprice (0), stopprice (0);
if c[1] > c[0] AND c[0] > c[3] AND c[3] > c[2] then begin
Buy Next Bar at open;
if Marketposition = 0 then begin
profitprice = O of tomorrow * (1+ptarget/100);
stopprice = O of tomorrow * (1-stopl/100);
sell next bar at profitprice limit;
sell next bar at stopprice stop;
end;
end;
if marketposition= 1 then begin
profitprice= entryprice * (1 + ptarget/100);
stopprice= entryprice * (1 - stopl/100);
sell next bar at profitprice limit;
sell next bar at stopprice stop;
end;

{File:QQQQ.txt Index:6 Index Date:20050120 PL:68.57% PS:
31.43% Trades:35 CL:3}
{LONG, %, TARGET: 7, STOP: 7, ENTRY PRICE: OPEN, DELAY: 0}
input: ptarget (7), stopl (7);
variables: profitprice (0), stopprice (0);
if c[2] > c[3] AND c[3] > c[1] AND c[1] > c[4] AND c[4] >
c[0] then begin
Buy Next Bar at open;
if Marketposition = 0 then begin
profitprice = O of tomorrow * (1+ptarget/100);
stopprice = O of tomorrow * (1-stopl/100);
sell next bar at profitprice limit;
```

```
sell next bar at stopprice stop;
end;
end;
if marketposition= 1 then begin
profitprice= entryprice * (1 + ptarget/100);
stopprice= entryprice * (1 - stopl/100);
sell next bar at profitprice limit;
sell next bar at stopprice stop;
end;


{File:QQQQ.txt Index:2 Index Date:20050218 PL:68.57% PS:
31.43% Trades:35 CL:3}
{LONG, %, TARGET: 7, STOP: 7, ENTRY PRICE: OPEN, DELAY: 0}
input: ptarget (7), stopl (7);
variables: profitprice (0), stopprice (0);
if h[2] > h[1] AND h[1] > c[2] AND c[2] > l[2] AND l[2] >
h[0] AND h[0] > c[1] AND c[1] > l[1] AND l[1] > c[0] AND
c[0] > l[0] then begin
Buy Next Bar at open;
if Marketposition = 0 then begin
profitprice = O of tomorrow * (1+ptarget/100);
stopprice = O of tomorrow * (1-stopl/100);
sell next bar at profitprice limit;
sell next bar at stopprice stop;
end;
end;
if marketposition= 1 then begin
profitprice= entryprice * (1 + ptarget/100);
stopprice= entryprice * (1 - stopl/100);
sell next bar at profitprice limit;
sell next bar at stopprice stop;
end;


{File:QQQQ.txt Index:4 Index Date:20040430 PL:68.52% PS:
31.48% Trades:54 CL:3}
{LONG, %, TARGET: 7, STOP: 7, ENTRY PRICE: OPEN, DELAY: 0}
input: ptarget (7), stopl (7);
variables: profitprice (0), stopprice (0);
if h[3] > h[2] AND h[2] > l[3] AND l[3] > h[1] AND h[1] >
l[2] AND l[2] > h[0] AND h[0] > l[1] AND l[1] > l[0] then
begin
Buy Next Bar at open;
if Marketposition = 0 then begin
profitprice = O of tomorrow * (1+ptarget/100);
stopprice = O of tomorrow * (1-stopl/100);
sell next bar at profitprice limit;
```

```
sell next bar at stopprice stop;
end;
end;
if marketposition= 1 then begin
profitprice= entryprice * (1 + ptarget/100);
stopprice= entryprice * (1 - stopl/100);
sell next bar at profitprice limit;
sell next bar at stopprice stop;
end;

{File:QQQQ.txt Index:12 Index Date:20041111 PL:68.09% PS:
31.91% Trades:47 CL:3}
{LONG, %, TARGET: 7, STOP: 7, ENTRY PRICE: OPEN, DELAY: 0}
input: ptarget (7), stopl (7);
variables: profitprice (0), stopprice (0);
if h[0] > l[3] AND l[3] > l[2] AND l[2] > l[1] AND l[1] >
l[4] then begin
Buy Next Bar at open;
if Marketposition = 0 then begin
profitprice = O of tomorrow * (1+ptarget/100);
stopprice = O of tomorrow * (1-stopl/100);
sell next bar at profitprice limit;
sell next bar at stopprice stop;
end;
end;
if marketposition= 1 then begin
profitprice= entryprice * (1 + ptarget/100);
stopprice= entryprice * (1 - stopl/100);
sell next bar at profitprice limit;
sell next bar at stopprice stop;
end;

{File:QQQQ.txt Index:4 Index Date:20041203 PL:67.27% PS:
32.73% Trades:55 CL:3}
{LONG, %, TARGET: 7, STOP: 7, ENTRY PRICE: OPEN, DELAY: 0}
{The value of the input variables must be specified in
 Tradestation}
input: ptarget (7), stopl (7);
variables: profitprice (0), stopprice (0);
if h[0] > h[1] AND h[1] > l[0] AND l[0] > h[2] AND h[2] >
 l[1] AND l[1] > h[3] AND h[3] > l[2] AND l[2] > l[3]
 then begin
Buy Next Bar at open;
if Marketposition = 0 then begin
profitprice = O of tomorrow * (1+ptarget/100);
stopprice = O of tomorrow * (1-stopl/100);
sell next bar at profitprice limit;
```

```
sell next bar at stopprice stop;
end;
end;
if marketposition= 1 then begin
profitprice= entryprice * (1 + ptarget/100);
stopprice= entryprice * (1 - stopl/100);
sell next bar at profitprice limit;
sell next bar at stopprice stop;
end;
```

3. Wealth-Lab Script   Wealth-lab code for selected QQQQ patterns. Wealth-Lab is a trademark of WL Systems, Inc.

```
// File:QQQQ.txt Index:1 Index Date:20050218 PL:67.57% PS:
32.43% Trades:37 CL:3
// LONG, %, TARGET: 7, STOP: 7, ENTRY PRICE: OPEN, DELAY: 0
var Bar: integer;
SetAutoStopMode (#AsPercent);
InstallProfitTarget (7);
InstallStopLoss (7);
for Bar:= 12 to BarCount - 1 do
begin
if not LastPositionActive then begin
if (PriceHigh (Bar-1) > PriceOpen (Bar-1)) AND (PriceOpen
(Bar-1) > PriceHigh (Bar-0)) AND (PriceHigh (Bar-0) >
PriceOpen (Bar-0)) AND (PriceOpen (Bar-0) > PriceClose
(Bar-1)) AND (PriceClose (Bar-1) > PriceLow (Bar-1)) AND
(PriceLow (Bar-1) > PriceClose (Bar-0)) AND (PriceClose
(Bar-0) > PriceLow (Bar-0)) then
BuyAtMarket (Bar+1, 'Open');
end
else
ApplyAutoStops (Bar);
end;


// File:QQQQ.txt Index:11 Index Date:20041012 PL:71.43% PS:
28.57% Trades:35 CL:3
// LONG, %, TARGET: 7, STOP: 7, ENTRY PRICE: OPEN, DELAY: 0
var Bar: integer;
SetAutoStopMode (#AsPercent);
InstallProfitTarget (7);
InstallStopLoss (7);
for Bar:= 12 to BarCount - 1 do
begin
if not LastPositionActive then begin
if (PriceLow (Bar-3) > PriceHigh (Bar-0)) AND (PriceHigh
```

```
(Bar-0) > PriceLow (Bar-1)) AND (PriceLow (Bar-1) >
PriceLow (Bar-2)) then
BuyAtMarket (Bar+1, 'Open');
end
else
ApplyAutoStops (Bar);
end;


// File:QQQQ.txt Index:7 Index Date:20041101 PL:70.97% PS:
29.03% Trades:31 CL:2
// LONG, %, TARGET: 7, STOP: 7, ENTRY PRICE: OPEN, DELAY: 0
var Bar: integer;
SetAutoStopMode (#AsPercent);
InstallProfitTarget (7);
InstallStopLoss (7);
for Bar:= 12 to BarCount - 1 do
begin
if not LastPositionActive then begin
if (PriceClose (Bar-0) > PriceClose (Bar-2)) AND
(PriceClose (Bar-2) > PriceClose (Bar-1)) AND (PriceClose
(Bar-1) > PriceClose (Bar-3)) AND (PriceClose (Bar-3) >
PriceClose (Bar-4)) AND (PriceClose (Bar-4) > PriceClose
(Bar-5)) then
BuyAtMarket (Bar+1, 'Open');
end
else
ApplyAutoStops (Bar);
end;


// File:QQQQ.txt Index:7 Index Date:20041001 PL:70.59% PS:
29.41% Trades:34 CL:2
// LONG, %, TARGET: 7, STOP: 7, ENTRY PRICE: OPEN, DELAY: 0
var Bar: integer;
SetAutoStopMode (#AsPercent);
InstallProfitTarget (7);
InstallStopLoss (7);
for Bar:= 12 to BarCount - 1 do
begin
if not LastPositionActive then begin
if (PriceClose (Bar-0) > PriceClose (Bar-1)) AND
(PriceClose (Bar-1) > PriceClose (Bar-2)) AND (PriceClose
(Bar-2) > PriceClose (Bar-5)) AND (PriceClose (Bar-5) >
PriceClose (Bar-3)) AND (PriceClose (Bar-3) > PriceClose
(Bar-4)) then
BuyAtMarket (Bar+1, 'Open');
end;
```

```
else
ApplyAutoStops (Bar);
end;

// File:QQQQ.txt Index:5 Index Date:20050207 PL:69.09% PS:
30.91% Trades:55 CL:2
// LONG, %, TARGET: 7, STOP: 7, ENTRY PRICE: OPEN, DELAY: 0
var Bar: integer;
SetAutoStopMode (#AsPercent);
InstallProfitTarget (7);
InstallStopLoss (7);
for Bar:= 12 to BarCount - 1 do
begin
if not LastPositionActive then begin
if (PriceClose (Bar-1) > PriceClose (Bar-0)) AND
(PriceClose (Bar-0) > PriceClose (Bar-3)) AND (PriceClose
(Bar-3) > PriceClose (Bar-2)) then
BuyAtMarket (Bar+1, 'Open');
end
else
ApplyAutoStops (Bar);
end;

// File:QQQQ.txt Index:6 Index Date:20050120 PL:68.57% PS:
31.43% Trades:35 CL:3
// LONG, %, TARGET: 7, STOP: 7, ENTRY PRICE: OPEN, DELAY: 0
var Bar: integer;
SetAutoStopMode (#AsPercent);
InstallProfitTarget (7);
InstallStopLoss (7);
for Bar:= 12 to BarCount - 1 do
begin
if not LastPositionActive then begin
if (PriceClose (Bar-2) > PriceClose (Bar-3)) AND
(PriceClose (Bar-3) > PriceClose (Bar-1)) AND (PriceClose
(Bar-1) > PriceClose (Bar-4)) AND (PriceClose (Bar-4) >
PriceClose (Bar-0)) then
BuyAtMarket (Bar+1, 'Open');
end;
else
ApplyAutoStops (Bar);
end;

// File:QQQQ.txt Index:2 Index Date:20050218 PL:68.57% PS:
31.43% Trades:35 CL:3
// LONG, %, TARGET: 7, STOP: 7, ENTRY PRICE: OPEN, DELAY: 0
var Bar: integer;
```

```
SetAutoStopMode (#AsPercent);
InstallProfitTarget (7);
InstallStopLoss (7);
for Bar:= 12 to BarCount - 1 do
begin
if not LastPositionActive then begin
if (PriceHigh (Bar-2) > PriceHigh (Bar-1)) AND (PriceHigh
(Bar-1) > PriceClose (Bar-2)) AND (PriceClose (Bar-2) >
PriceLow (Bar-2)) AND (PriceLow (Bar-2) > PriceHigh
(Bar-0)) AND (PriceHigh (Bar-0) > PriceClose (Bar-1)) AND
(PriceClose (Bar-1) > PriceLow (Bar-1)) AND (PriceLow
(Bar-1) > PriceClose (Bar-0)) AND (PriceClose (Bar-0) >
PriceLow (Bar-0)) then
BuyAtMarket (Bar+1, 'Open');
end;
else
ApplyAutoStops (Bar);
end;

// File:QQQQ.txt Index:4 Index Date:20040430 PL:68.52% PS:
31.48% Trades:54 CL:3
// LONG, %, TARGET: 7, STOP: 7, ENTRY PRICE: OPEN, DELAY: 0
var Bar: integer;
SetAutoStopMode (#AsPercent);
InstallProfitTarget (7);
InstallStopLoss (7);
for Bar:= 12 to BarCount - 1 do
begin
if not LastPositionActive then begin
if (PriceHigh (Bar-3) > PriceHigh (Bar-2)) AND (PriceHigh
(Bar-2) > PriceLow (Bar-3)) AND (PriceLow (Bar-3) >
PriceHigh (Bar-1)) AND (PriceHigh (Bar-1) > PriceLow
(Bar-2)) AND (PriceLow (Bar-2) > PriceHigh (Bar-0)) AND
(PriceHigh (Bar-0) > PriceLow (Bar-1)) AND (PriceLow
(Bar-1) > PriceLow (Bar-0)) then
BuyAtMarket (Bar+1, 'Open');
end;
else
ApplyAutoStops (Bar);
end;

// File:QQQQ.txt Index:12 Index Date:20041111 PL:68.09% PS:
31.91% Trades:47 CL:3
// LONG, %, TARGET: 7, STOP: 7, ENTRY PRICE: OPEN, DELAY: 0
var Bar: integer;
SetAutoStopMode (#AsPercent);
InstallProfitTarget (7);
```

```
InstallStopLoss (7);
for Bar:= 12 to BarCount - 1 do
begin
if not LastPositionActive then begin
if (PriceHigh (Bar-0) > PriceLow (Bar-3)) AND (PriceLow
(Bar-3) > PriceLow (Bar-2)) AND (PriceLow (Bar-2) >
PriceLow (Bar-1)) AND (PriceLow (Bar-1) > PriceLow (Bar-4))
then
BuyAtMarket (Bar+1, 'Open');
end
else
ApplyAutoStops (Bar);
end;


// File:QQQQ.txt Index:4 Index Date:20041203 PL:67.27% PS:
32.73% Trades:55 CL:3
// LONG, %, TARGET: 7, STOP: 7, ENTRY PRICE: OPEN, DELAY: 0
var Bar: integer;
SetAutoStopMode (#AsPercent);
InstallProfitTarget (7);
InstallStopLoss (7);
for Bar:= 12 to BarCount - 1 do
begin
if not LastPositionActive then begin
if (PriceHigh (Bar-0) > PriceHigh (Bar-1)) AND (PriceHigh
(Bar-1) > PriceLow (Bar-0)) AND (PriceLow (Bar-0) >
PriceHigh (Bar-2)) AND (PriceHigh (Bar-2) > PriceLow
(Bar-1)) AND (PriceLow (Bar-1) > PriceHigh (Bar-3)) AND
(PriceHigh (Bar-3) > PriceLow (Bar-2)) AND (PriceLow
(Bar-2) > PriceLow (Bar-3)) then
BuyAtMarket (Bar+1, 'Open');
end
else
ApplyAutoStops (Bar);
end;
```

SPY Patterns

1. Metastock Formula Code   Metastock code for selected SPY patterns. Metastock® is a registered trademark of Equis International, a Reuters company.

```
{File:SPY.txt Index:2 Index Date:20070807 PL:74.19% PS:
25.81% Trades:31 CL:2}
{LONG, %, TARGET : 7, STOP : 7, ENTRY PRICE : OPEN, DELAY
: 1}
```

```
(Ref(h,0) > Ref(c,0)) AND (Ref(c,0) > Ref(h,-2)) AND
(Ref(h,-2) > Ref(h,-1)) AND (Ref(h,-1) > Ref(l,0)) AND
(Ref(l,0) > Ref(l,-2)) AND (Ref(l,-2) > Ref(l,-1))

{File:SPY.txt Index:2 Index Date:20070703 PL:67.74% PS:
32.26% Trades:31 CL:2}
{LONG, %, TARGET : 7, STOP : 7, ENTRY PRICE : OPEN, DELAY
: 1}
(Ref(h,0) > Ref(c,0)) AND (Ref(c,0) > Ref(l,0)) AND
(Ref(l,0) > Ref(h,-1)) AND (Ref(h,-1) > Ref(h,-2)) AND
(Ref(h,-2) > Ref(l,-1)) AND (Ref(l,-1) > Ref(l,-2))

{File:SPY.txt Index:10 Index Date:20061101 PL:77.42% PS:
22.58% Trades:31 CL:2}
{LONG, %, TARGET : 7, STOP : 7, ENTRY PRICE : OPEN, DELAY :
1}
(Ref(c,-4) > Ref(c,-5)) AND (Ref(c,-5) > Ref(c,-3)) AND
(Ref(c,-3) > Ref(c,-2)) AND (Ref(c,-2) > Ref(c,-1)) AND
(Ref(c,-1) > Ref(c,0))

{File:SPY.txt Index:8 Index Date:20070511 PL:67.74% PS:
32.26% Trades:31 CL:3}
{LONG, %, TARGET : 7, STOP : 7, ENTRY PRICE : OPEN, DELAY :
1}
(Ref(c,-2) > Ref(c,0)) AND (Ref(c,0) > Ref(c,-3)) AND
(Ref(c,-3) > Ref(c,-1))

{File:SPY.txt Index:9 Index Date:20070808 PL:78.79% PS:
21.21% Trades:33 CL:2}
{LONG, %, TARGET : 7, STOP : 7, ENTRY PRICE : OPEN, DELAY :
1}
(Ref(c,0) > Ref(c,-1)) AND (Ref(c,-1) > Ref(c,-4)) AND
(Ref(c,-4) > Ref(c,-2)) AND (Ref(c,-2) > Ref(c,-3))

{File:SPY.txt Index:2 Index Date:20070724 PL:78.79% PS:
21.21% Trades:33 CL:3}
{LONG, %, TARGET : 7, STOP : 7, ENTRY PRICE : OPEN, DELAY :
1}
(Ref(h,-2) > Ref(h,-1)) AND (Ref(h,-1) > Ref(h,0)) AND
(Ref(h,0) > Ref(l,-1)) AND (Ref(l,-1) > Ref(l,-2)) AND
(Ref(l,-2) > Ref(c,0)) AND (Ref(c,0) > Ref(l,0))

{File:SPY.txt Index:2 Index Date:20070327 PL:67.65% PS:
32.35% Trades:34 CL:3}
{LONG, %, TARGET : 7, STOP : 7, ENTRY PRICE : OPEN, DELAY :
1}
(Ref(h,-2) > Ref(h,-1)) AND (Ref(h,-1) > Ref(h,0)) AND
(Ref(h,0) > Ref(l,-2)) AND (Ref(l,-2) > Ref(c,0)) AND
```

(Ref(c,0) > Ref(l,0)) AND (Ref(l,0) > Ref(l,-1))

{File:SPY.txt Index:1 Index Date:20070703 PL:70.59% PS:
29.41% Trades:34 CL:2}
{LONG, %, TARGET : 7, STOP : 7, ENTRY PRICE : OPEN, DELAY :
1}
(Ref(h,0) > Ref(l,0)) AND (Ref(l,0) > Ref(h,-1)) AND
(Ref(h,-1) > Ref(h,-2)) AND (Ref(h,-2) > Ref(l,-1)) AND
(Ref(l,-1) > Ref(l,-2))

{File:SPY.txt Index:1 Index Date:20070621 PL:77.78% PS:
22.22% Trades:36 CL:3}
{LONG, %, TARGET : 7, STOP : 7, ENTRY PRICE : OPEN, DELAY :
1}
(Ref(h,-1) > Ref(h,-2)) AND (Ref(h,-2) > Ref(l,-2)) AND
(Ref(l,-2) > Ref(h,0)) AND (Ref(h,0) > Ref(l,-1)) AND
(Ref(l,-1) > Ref(l,0))

{File:SPY.txt Index:1 Index Date:20070424 PL:83.33% PS:
16.67% Trades:36 CL:2}
{LONG, %, TARGET : 7, STOP : 7, ENTRY PRICE : OPEN, DELAY :
1}
(Ref(h,-1) > Ref(h,-2)) AND (Ref(h,-2) > Ref(h,0)) AND
(Ref(h,0) > Ref(l,-1)) AND (Ref(l,-1) > Ref(l,0)) AND
(Ref(l,0) > Ref(l,-2))

{File:SPY.txt Index:2 Index Date:20070807 PL:74.19% PS:
25.81% Trades:31 CL:2}
{LONG, %, TARGET : 7, STOP : 7, ENTRY PRICE : OPEN, DELAY :
1}
(Ref(h,0) > Ref(c,0)) AND (Ref(c,0) > Ref(h,-2)) AND
(Ref(h,-2) > Ref(h,-1)) AND (Ref(h,-1) > Ref(l,0)) AND
(Ref(l,0) > Ref(l,-2)) AND (Ref(l,-2) > Ref(l,-1))

{File:SPY.txt Index:2 Index Date:20070703 PL:67.74% PS:
32.26% Trades:31 CL:2}
{LONG, %, TARGET : 7, STOP : 7, ENTRY PRICE : OPEN, DELAY :
1}
(Ref(h,0) > Ref(c,0)) AND (Ref(c,0) > Ref(l,0)) AND
(Ref(l,0) > Ref(h,-1)) AND (Ref(h,-1) > Ref(h,-2)) AND
(Ref(h,-2) > Ref(l,-1)) AND (Ref(l,-1) > Ref(l,-2))

{File:SPY.txt Index:10 Index Date:20061101 PL:77.42% PS:
22.58% Trades:31 CL:2}
{LONG, %, TARGET : 7, STOP : 7, ENTRY PRICE : OPEN, DELAY :
1}
(Ref(c,-4) > Ref(c,-5)) AND (Ref(c,-5) > Ref(c,-3)) AND

```
(Ref(c,-3) > Ref(c,-2)) AND (Ref(c,-2) > Ref(c,-1)) AND
(Ref(c,-1) > Ref(c,0))


{File:SPY.txt Index:8 Index Date:20070511 PL:67.74% PS:
32.26% Trades:31 CL:3}
{LONG, %, TARGET : 7, STOP : 7, ENTRY PRICE : OPEN, DELAY :
1}
(Ref(c,-2) > Ref(c,0)) AND (Ref(c,0) > Ref(c,-3)) AND
(Ref(c,-3) > Ref(c,-1))


{File:SPY.txt Index:9 Index Date:20070808 PL:78.79% PS:
21.21% Trades:33 CL:2}
{LONG, %, TARGET : 7, STOP : 7, ENTRY PRICE : OPEN, DELAY :
1}
(Ref(c,0) > Ref(c,-1)) AND (Ref(c,-1) > Ref(c,-4)) AND
(Ref(c,-4) > Ref(c,-2)) AND (Ref(c,-2) > Ref(c,-3))


{File:SPY.txt Index:2 Index Date:20070724 PL:78.79% PS:
21.21% Trades:33 CL:3}
{LONG, %, TARGET : 7, STOP : 7, ENTRY PRICE : OPEN, DELAY :
1}
(Ref(h,-2) > Ref(h,-1)) AND (Ref(h,-1) > Ref(h,0)) AND
(Ref(h,0) > Ref(l,-1)) AND (Ref(l,-1) > Ref(l,-2)) AND
(Ref(l,-2) > Ref(c,0)) AND (Ref(c,0) > Ref(l,0))


{File:SPY.txt Index:2 Index Date:20070327 PL:67.65% PS:
32.35% Trades:34 CL:3}
{LONG, %, TARGET : 7, STOP : 7, ENTRY PRICE : OPEN, DELAY :
1}
(Ref(h,-2) > Ref(h,-1)) AND (Ref(h,-1) > Ref(h,0)) AND
(Ref(h,0) > Ref(l,-2)) AND (Ref(l,-2) > Ref(c,0)) AND
(Ref(c,0) > Ref(l,0)) AND (Ref(l,0) > Ref(l,-1))


{File:SPY.txt Index:1 Index Date:20070703 PL:70.59% PS:
29.41% Trades:34 CL:2}
{LONG, %, TARGET : 7, STOP : 7, ENTRY PRICE : OPEN, DELAY :
1}
(Ref(h,0) > Ref(l,0)) AND (Ref(l,0) > Ref(h,-1)) AND
(Ref(h,-1) > Ref(h,-2)) AND (Ref(h,-2) > Ref(l,-1)) AND
(Ref(l,-1) > Ref(l,-2))


{File:SPY.txt Index:1 Index Date:20070621 PL:77.78% PS:
22.22% Trades:36 CL:3}
{LONG, %, TARGET : 7, STOP : 7, ENTRY PRICE : OPEN, DELAY :
1}
(Ref(h,-1) > Ref(h,-2)) AND (Ref(h,-2) > Ref(l,-2)) AND
```

```
(Ref(l,-2) > Ref(h,0)) AND (Ref(h,0) > Ref(l,-1)) AND
(Ref(l,-1) > Ref(l,0))

{File:SPY.txt Index:1 Index Date:20070424 PL:83.33% PS:
16.67% Trades:36 CL:2}
{LONG, %, TARGET : 7, STOP : 7, ENTRY PRICE : OPEN, DELAY :
1}
(Ref(h,-1) > Ref(h,-2)) AND (Ref(h,-2) > Ref(h,0)) AND
(Ref(h,0) > Ref(l,-1)) AND (Ref(l,-1) > Ref(l,0)) AND
(Ref(l,0) > Ref(l,-2))
```

2. EasyLanguage Code
EasyLanguage® code for selected SPY patterns. EasyLanguage® is a registered trademark of TradeStation Technologies, Inc.

```
{File:SPY.txt Index:2 Index Date:20070807 PL:74.19% PS:
25.81% Trades:31 CL:2}
{LONG, %, TARGET : 7, STOP : 7, ENTRY PRICE : OPEN, DELAY :
0}
input: ptarget(7), stopl(7);
variables: profitprice(0), stopprice(0);
if h[0] > c[0] AND c[0] > h[2] AND h[2] > h[1] AND h[1] >
l[0] AND l[0] > l[2] AND l[2] > l[1] then begin
Buy Next Bar at open;
if Marketposition = 0 then begin
profitprice = O of tomorrow * (1+ptarget/100);
stopprice = O of tomorrow * (1-stopl/100);
sell next bar at profitprice limit;
sell next bar at stopprice stop;
end;
end;
if marketposition= 1 then begin
profitprice= entryprice * (1 + ptarget/100);
stopprice= entryprice * (1 - stopl/100);
sell next bar at profitprice limit;
sell next bar at stopprice stop;
end;

File:SPY.txt Index:2 Index Date:20070703 PL:67.74% PS:32.26%
Trades:31 CL:2}
{LONG, %, TARGET : 7, STOP : 7, ENTRY PRICE : OPEN, DELAY :
0}
input: ptarget(7), stopl(7);
variables: profitprice(0), stopprice(0);
if h[0] > c[0] AND c[0] > l[0] AND l[0] > h[1] AND h[1] >
```

```
h[2] AND h[2] > l[1] AND l[1] > l[2] then begin
Buy Next Bar at open;
if Marketposition = 0 then begin
profitprice = O of tomorrow * (1+ptarget/100);
stopprice = O of tomorrow * (1-stopl/100);
sell next bar at profitprice limit;
sell next bar at stopprice stop;
end;
end;
if marketposition= 1 then begin
profitprice= entryprice * (1 + ptarget/100);
stopprice= entryprice * (1 - stopl/100);
sell next bar at profitprice limit;
sell next bar at stopprice stop;
end;

{File:SPY.txt Index:10 Index Date:20061101 PL:77.42% PS:
22.58% Trades:31 CL:2}
{LONG, %, TARGET : 7, STOP : 7, ENTRY PRICE : OPEN, DELAY :
0}
input: ptarget(7), stopl(7);
variables: profitprice(0), stopprice(0);
if c[4] > c[5] AND c[5] > c[3] AND c[3] > c[2] AND c[2] >
c[1] AND c[1] > c[0] then begin
Buy Next Bar at open;
if Marketposition = 0 then begin
profitprice = O of tomorrow * (1+ptarget/100);
stopprice = O of tomorrow * (1-stopl/100);
sell next bar at profitprice limit;
sell next bar at stopprice stop;
end;
end;
if marketposition= 1 then begin
profitprice= entryprice * (1 + ptarget/100);
stopprice= entryprice * (1 - stopl/100);
sell next bar at profitprice limit;
sell next bar at stopprice stop;
end;

{File:SPY.txt Index:8 Index Date:20070511 PL:67.74% PS:
32.26% Trades:31 CL:3}
{LONG, %, TARGET : 7, STOP : 7, ENTRY PRICE : OPEN, DELAY :
0}
input: ptarget(7), stopl(7);
variables: profitprice(0), stopprice(0);
if c[2] > c[0] AND c[0] > c[3] AND c[3] > c[1] then begin
```

```
Buy Next Bar at open;
if Marketposition = 0 then begin
profitprice = O of tomorrow * (1+ptarget/100);
stopprice = O of tomorrow * (1-stopl/100);
sell next bar at profitprice limit;
sell next bar at stopprice stop;
end;
end;
if marketposition= 1 then begin
profitprice= entryprice * (1 + ptarget/100);
stopprice= entryprice * (1 - stopl/100);
sell next bar at profitprice limit;
sell next bar at stopprice stop;
end;

{File:SPY.txt Index:9 Index Date:20070808 PL:78.79% PS:
21.21% Trades:33 CL:2}
{LONG, %, TARGET : 7, STOP : 7, ENTRY PRICE : OPEN,
DELAY : 0}
input: ptarget(7), stopl(7);
variables: profitprice(0), stopprice(0);
if c[0] > c[1] AND c[1] > c[4] AND c[4] > c[2] AND c[2] >
c[3] then begin
Buy Next Bar at open;
if Marketposition = 0 then begin
profitprice = O of tomorrow * (1+ptarget/100);
stopprice = O of tomorrow * (1-stopl/100);
sell next bar at profitprice limit;
sell next bar at stopprice stop;
end;
end;
if marketposition= 1 then begin
profitprice= entryprice * (1 + ptarget/100);
stopprice= entryprice * (1 - stopl/100);
sell next bar at profitprice limit;
sell next bar at stopprice stop;
end;

{File:SPY.txt Index:2 Index Date:20070724 PL:78.79% PS:
21.21% Trades:33 CL:3}
{LONG, %, TARGET : 7, STOP : 7, ENTRY PRICE : OPEN, DELAY :
0}
input: ptarget(7), stopl(7);
variables: profitprice(0), stopprice(0);
if h[2] > h[1] AND h[1] > h[0] AND h[0] > l[1] AND l[1] >
l[2] AND l[2] > c[0] AND c[0] > l[0] then begin
```

```
Buy Next Bar at open;
if Marketposition = 0 then begin
profitprice = O of tomorrow * (1+ptarget/100);
stopprice = O of tomorrow * (1-stopl/100);
sell next bar at profitprice limit;
sell next bar at stopprice stop;
end;
end;
if marketposition= 1 then begin
profitprice= entryprice * (1 + ptarget/100);
stopprice= entryprice * (1 - stopl/100);
sell next bar at profitprice limit;
sell next bar at stopprice stop;
end;

{File:SPY.txt Index:2 Index Date:20070327 PL:67.65% PS:
32.35% Trades:34 CL:3}
{LONG, %, TARGET : 7, STOP : 7, ENTRY PRICE : OPEN, DELAY :
0}
input: ptarget(7), stopl(7);
variables: profitprice(0), stopprice(0);
if h[2] > h[1] AND h[1] > h[0] AND h[0] > l[2] AND l[2] >
c[0] AND c[0] > l[0] AND l[0] > l[1] then begin
Buy Next Bar at open;
if Marketposition = 0 then begin
profitprice = O of tomorrow * (1+ptarget/100);
stopprice = O of tomorrow * (1-stopl/100);
sell next bar at profitprice limit;
sell next bar at stopprice stop;
end;
end;
if marketposition= 1 then begin
profitprice= entryprice * (1 + ptarget/100);
stopprice= entryprice * (1 - stopl/100);
sell next bar at profitprice limit;
sell next bar at stopprice stop;
end;

{File:SPY.txt Index:1 Index Date:20070703 PL:70.59% PS:
29.41% Trades:34 CL:2}
{LONG, %, TARGET : 7, STOP : 7, ENTRY PRICE : OPEN, DELAY :
0}
input: ptarget(7), stopl(7);
variables: profitprice(0), stopprice(0);
if h[0] > l[0] AND l[0] > h[1] AND h[1] > h[2] AND h[2] >
l[1] AND l[1] > l[2] then begin
```

```
Buy Next Bar at open;
if Marketposition = 0 then begin
profitprice = O of tomorrow * (1+ptarget/100);
stopprice = O of tomorrow * (1-stopl/100);
sell next bar at profitprice limit;
sell next bar at stopprice stop;
end;
end;
if marketposition= 1 then begin
profitprice= entryprice * (1 + ptarget/100);
stopprice= entryprice * (1 - stopl/100);
sell next bar at profitprice limit;
sell next bar at stopprice stop;
end;

{File:SPY.txt Index:1 Index Date:20070621 PL:77.78% PS:
22.22% Trades:36 CL:3}
{LONG, %, TARGET : 7, STOP : 7, ENTRY PRICE : OPEN, DELAY :
0}
input: ptarget(7), stopl(7);
variables: profitprice(0), stopprice(0);
if h[1] > h[2] AND h[2] > l[2] AND l[2] > h[0] AND h[0] >
l[1] AND l[1] > l[0] then begin
Buy Next Bar at open;
if Marketposition = 0 then begin
profitprice = O of tomorrow * (1+ptarget/100);
stopprice = O of tomorrow * (1-stopl/100);
sell next bar at profitprice limit;
sell next bar at stopprice stop;
end;
end;
if marketposition= 1 then begin
profitprice= entryprice * (1 + ptarget/100);
stopprice= entryprice * (1 - stopl/100);
sell next bar at profitprice limit;
sell next bar at stopprice stop;
end;

{File:SPY.txt Index:1 Index Date:20070424 PL:83.33% PS:
16.67% Trades:36 CL:2}
{LONG, %, TARGET : 7, STOP : 7, ENTRY PRICE : OPEN, DELAY :
0}
input: ptarget(7), stopl(7);
variables: profitprice(0), stopprice(0);
if h[1] > h[2] AND h[2] > h[0] AND h[0] > l[1] AND l[1] >
l[0] AND l[0] > l[2] then begin
```

```
Buy Next Bar at open;
if Marketposition = 0 then begin
profitprice = O of tomorrow * (1+ptarget/100);
stopprice = O of tomorrow * (1-stopl/100);
sell next bar at profitprice limit;
sell next bar at stopprice stop;
end;
end;
if marketposition= 1 then begin
profitprice= entryprice * (1 + ptarget/100);
stopprice= entryprice * (1 - stopl/100);
sell next bar at profitprice limit;
sell next bar at stopprice stop;
end;
```

3. Wealth-Lab Script Wealth-lab code for selected SPY patterns.
Wealth-Lab is a trademark of WL Systems, Inc.

```
// File:SPY.txt   Index:2   Index Date:20070807   PL:74.19%
PS:25.81%  Trades:31  CL:2
// LONG, %, TARGET : 7, STOP : 7, ENTRY PRICE : OPEN, DELAY
: 0
var Bar: integer;
SetAutoStopMode(#AsPercent);
InstallProfitTarget(7);
InstallStopLoss(7);
for Bar := 12 to BarCount - 1 do
begin
if not LastPositionActive then begin
if (PriceHigh(Bar-0) > PriceClose(Bar-0)) AND
(PriceClose(Bar-0) > PriceHigh(Bar-2)) AND
(PriceHigh(Bar-2) > PriceHigh(Bar-1)) AND (PriceHigh(Bar-1)
> PriceLow(Bar-0)) AND (PriceLow(Bar-0) > PriceLow(Bar-2))
AND (PriceLow(Bar-2) > PriceLow(Bar-1)) then
BuyAtMarket(Bar+1, 'Open');
end
else
ApplyAutoStops(Bar);
end;


// File:SPY.txt Index:2 Index Date:20070703 PL:67.74% PS:
32.26% Trades:31 CL:2
// LONG, %, TARGET : 7, STOP : 7, ENTRY PRICE : OPEN, DELAY
: 0
var Bar: integer;
SetAutoStopMode(#AsPercent);
```

```
InstallProfitTarget(7);
InstallStopLoss(7);
for Bar := 12 to BarCount - 1 do
begin
if not LastPositionActive then begin
if (PriceHigh(Bar-0) > PriceClose(Bar-0)) AND
(PriceClose(Bar-0) > PriceLow(Bar-0)) AND (PriceLow(Bar-0)
> PriceHigh(Bar-1)) AND (PriceHigh(Bar-1) >
PriceHigh(Bar-2)) AND (PriceHigh(Bar-2) > PriceLow(Bar-1))
AND (PriceLow(Bar-1) > PriceLow(Bar-2)) then
BuyAtMarket(Bar+1, 'Open');
end
else
ApplyAutoStops(Bar);
end;

// File:SPY.txt Index:10 Index Date:20061101 PL:77.42% PS:
22.58% Trades:31 CL:2
// LONG, %, TARGET : 7, STOP : 7, ENTRY PRICE : OPEN, DELAY
: 0
var Bar: integer;
SetAutoStopMode(#AsPercent);
InstallProfitTarget(7);
InstallStopLoss(7);
for Bar := 12 to BarCount - 1 do
begin
if not LastPositionActive then begin
if (PriceClose(Bar-4) > PriceClose(Bar-5)) AND
(PriceClose(Bar-5) > PriceClose(Bar-3)) AND
(PriceClose(Bar-3) > PriceClose(Bar-2)) AND
(PriceClose(Bar-2) > PriceClose(Bar-1)) AND
(PriceClose(Bar-1) > PriceClose(Bar-0)) then
BuyAtMarket(Bar+1, 'Open');
end
else
ApplyAutoStops(Bar);
end;

// File:SPY.txt Index:8 Index Date:20070511 PL:67.74% PS:
32.26% Trades:31 CL:3
// LONG, %, TARGET : 7, STOP : 7, ENTRY PRICE : OPEN, DELAY
: 0
var Bar: integer;
SetAutoStopMode(#AsPercent);
InstallProfitTarget(7);
InstallStopLoss(7);
for Bar := 12 to BarCount - 1 do
```

```
begin
if not LastPositionActive then begin
if (PriceClose(Bar-2) > PriceClose(Bar-0)) AND
(PriceClose(Bar-0) > PriceClose(Bar-3)) AND
(PriceClose(Bar-3) > PriceClose(Bar-1)) then
BuyAtMarket(Bar+1, 'Open');
end
else
ApplyAutoStops(Bar);
end;

// File:SPY.txt Index:9 Index Date:20070808 PL:78.79% PS:
21.21% Trades:33 CL:2
// LONG, %, TARGET : 7, STOP : 7, ENTRY PRICE : OPEN, DELAY
: 0
var Bar: integer;
SetAutoStopMode(#AsPercent);
InstallProfitTarget(7);
InstallStopLoss(7);
for Bar := 12 to BarCount - 1 do
begin
if not LastPositionActive then begin
if (PriceClose(Bar-0) > PriceClose(Bar-1)) AND
(PriceClose(Bar-1) > PriceClose(Bar-4)) AND
(PriceClose(Bar-4) > PriceClose(Bar-2)) AND
(PriceClose(Bar-2) > PriceClose(Bar-3)) then
BuyAtMarket(Bar+1, 'Open');
end
else
ApplyAutoStops(Bar);
end;

// File:SPY.txt Index:2 Index Date:20070724 PL:78.79% PS:
21.21% Trades:33 CL:3
// LONG, %, TARGET : 7, STOP : 7, ENTRY PRICE : OPEN, DELAY
: 0
var Bar: integer;
SetAutoStopMode(#AsPercent);
InstallProfitTarget(7);
InstallStopLoss(7);
for Bar := 12 to BarCount - 1 do
begin
if not LastPositionActive then begin
if (PriceHigh(Bar-2) > PriceHigh(Bar-1)) AND
(PriceHigh(Bar-1) > PriceHigh(Bar-0)) AND (PriceHigh(Bar-0)
> PriceLow(Bar-1)) AND (PriceLow(Bar-1) > PriceLow(Bar-2))
```

```
AND (PriceLow(Bar-2) > PriceClose(Bar-0)) AND
(PriceClose(Bar-0) > PriceLow(Bar-0)) then
BuyAtMarket(Bar+1, 'Open');
end
else
ApplyAutoStops(Bar);
end;


// File:SPY.txt Index:2 Index Date:20070327 PL:67.65% PS:
32.35% Trades:34 CL:3
// LONG, %, TARGET : 7, STOP : 7, ENTRY PRICE : OPEN, DELAY
: 0
var Bar: integer;
SetAutoStopMode(#AsPercent);
InstallProfitTarget(7);
InstallStopLoss(7);
for Bar := 12 to BarCount - 1 do
begin
if not LastPositionActive then begin
if (PriceHigh(Bar-2) > PriceHigh(Bar-1)) AND
(PriceHigh(Bar-1) > PriceHigh(Bar-0)) AND (PriceHigh(Bar-0)
> PriceLow(Bar-2)) AND (PriceLow(Bar-2) >
PriceClose(Bar-0)) AND (PriceClose(Bar-0) >
PriceLow(Bar-0)) AND (PriceLow(Bar-0) >
PriceLow(Bar-1)) then
BuyAtMarket(Bar+1, 'Open');
end
else
ApplyAutoStops(Bar);
end;


// File:SPY.txt Index:1 Index Date:20070703 PL:70.59% PS:
29.41% Trades:34 CL:2
// LONG, %, TARGET : 7, STOP : 7, ENTRY PRICE : OPEN, DELAY
: 0
var Bar: integer;
SetAutoStopMode(#AsPercent);
InstallProfitTarget(7);
InstallStopLoss(7);
for Bar := 12 to BarCount - 1 do
begin
if not LastPositionActive then begin
if (PriceHigh(Bar-0) > PriceLow(Bar-0)) AND
(PriceLow(Bar-0) > PriceHigh(Bar-1)) AND (PriceHigh(Bar-1)
> PriceHigh(Bar-2)) AND (PriceHigh(Bar-2) >
 PriceLow(Bar-1)) AND (PriceLow(Bar-1) >
```

```
PriceLow(Bar-2)) then
BuyAtMarket(Bar+1, 'Open');
end
else
ApplyAutoStops(Bar);
end;


// File:SPY.txt Index:1 Index Date:20070621 PL:77.78% PS:
22.22% Trades:36 CL:3
// LONG, %, TARGET : 7, STOP : 7, ENTRY PRICE : OPEN, DELAY
: 0
var Bar: integer;
SetAutoStopMode(#AsPercent);
InstallProfitTarget(7);
InstallStopLoss(7);
for Bar := 12 to BarCount - 1 do
begin
if not LastPositionActive then begin
if (PriceHigh(Bar-1) > PriceHigh(Bar-2)) AND
(PriceHigh(Bar-2) > PriceLow(Bar-2)) AND (PriceLow(Bar-2)
> PriceHigh(Bar-0)) AND (PriceHigh(Bar-0) >
PriceLow(Bar-1)) AND (PriceLow(Bar-1) > PriceLow(Bar-0))
then
BuyAtMarket(Bar+1, 'Open');
end
else
ApplyAutoStops(Bar);
end;


// File:SPY.txt Index:1 Index Date:20070424 PL:83.33% PS:
16.67% Trades:36 CL:2
// LONG, %, TARGET : 7, STOP : 7, ENTRY PRICE : OPEN, DELAY
: 0
var Bar: integer;
SetAutoStopMode(#AsPercent);
InstallProfitTarget(7);
InstallStopLoss(7);
for Bar := 12 to BarCount - 1 do
begin
if not LastPositionActive then begin
if (PriceHigh(Bar-1) > PriceHigh(Bar-2)) AND
(PriceHigh(Bar-2) > PriceHigh(Bar-0)) AND (PriceHigh(Bar-0)
> PriceLow(Bar-1)) AND (PriceLow(Bar-1) > PriceLow(Bar-0))
AND (PriceLow(Bar-0) > PriceLow(Bar-2)) then
BuyAtMarket(Bar+1, 'Open');
end
```

```
else
ApplyAutoStops(Bar);
end;
```

DAX Patterns

1. Metastock Formula Code   Metastock code for selected DAX patterns. Metastock® is a registered trademark of Equis International, a Reuters company.

```
{File: DAX.txt Index: 11 Index Date: 20050121 PL: 68.42% PS:
31.58% Trades: 38 CL: 3}
{LONG, %, TARGET: 3, STOP: 3, ENTRY PRICE: OPEN, DELA: 1}
(Ref (l,-2) > Ref (h,0)) AND (Ref (h,0) > Ref (l,-3)) AND
(Ref (l,-3) > Ref (l,-1))

{File: DAX.txt Index: 10 Index Date: 20050331 PL: 32.26% PS:
67.74% Trades:31 CL: 2}
{SHORT, %, TARGET: 3, STOP: 3, ENTRY PRICE: OPEN, DELAY: 1}
(Ref (h,0) > Ref (h,-1)) AND (Ref (h,-1) > Ref (h,-2)) AND
(Ref (h,-2) > Ref (c,0)) AND (Ref (c,0) > Ref (l,0)) AND
(Ref (l,0) > Ref (l,-1)) AND (Ref (l,-1) > Ref (l,-2))

{File: DAX.txt Index: 6 Index Date: 20050223 PL: 15.63% PS:
84.38% Trades: 32 CL:1}
{SHORT, %, TARGET: 2, STOP: 4, ENTRY PRICE: OPEN, DELAY: 1}
(Ref (c,-4) > Ref (c,-2)) AND (Ref (c,-2) > Ref (c,-3)) AND
(Ref (c,-3) > Ref (c,-1)) AND (Ref (c,-1) > Ref (c,0))

{File: DAX.txt Index: 4 Index Date: 20050202 PL: 80.00% PS:
20.00% Trades: 30 CL:1}
{LONG, %, TARGET: 2, STOP: 4, ENTRY PRICE: OPEN, DELAY: 1}
(Ref (h,0) > Ref (h,-1)) AND (Ref (h,-1) > Ref (l,0)) AND
(Ref (l,0) > Ref (h,-2)) AND (Ref (h,-2) > Ref (l,-1)) AND
(Ref (l,-1) > Ref (h,-3)) AND (Ref (h,-3) > Ref (l,-2)) AND
(Ref (l,-2) > Ref (l,-3))
```

2. EasyLanguage Code   EasyLanguage® code for selected DAX patterns. EasyLanguage® is a registered trademark of TradeStation Technologies, Inc.

```
{File: DAX.txt Index: 11 Index Date: 20050121 PL: 68.42% PS:
31.58% Trades: 38 CL: 3}
{LONG, %, TARGET: 3, STOP: 3, ENTRY PRICE: OPEN, DELAY: 0}
```

```
input: ptarget (3), stopl (3);
variables: profitprice (0), stopprice (0);
if l[2] > h[0] AND h[0] > l[3] AND l[3] > l[1] then begin
Buy Next Bar at open;
if Marketposition = 0 then begin
profitprice = O of tomorrow * (1+ptarget/100);
stopprice = O of tomorrow * (1-stopl/100);
sell next bar at profitprice limit;
sell next bar at stopprice stop;
end;
end;
if marketposition= 1 then begin
profitprice= entryprice * (1 + ptarget/100);
stopprice= entryprice * (1 - stopl/100);
sell next bar at profitprice limit;
sell next bar at stopprice stop;
end;

{File: DAX.txt Index: 10 Index Date: 20050331 PL: 32.26% PS:
67.74% Trades: 31 CL: 2}
{SHORT, %, TARGET: 3, STOP: 3, ENTRY PRICE: OPEN, DELAY: 0}
input: ptarget (3), stopl (3);
variables: profitprice (0), stopprice (0);
if h[0] > h[1] AND h[1] > h[2] AND h[2] > c[0] AND c[0] >
l[0] AND l[0] > l[1] AND l[1] > l[2] then begin
Sell Short Next Bar at open;
if Marketposition = 0 then begin
profitprice = O of tomorrow * (1-ptarget/100);
stopprice = O of tomorrow * (1+stopl/100);
buy to cover next bar at profitprice limit;
buy to cover next bar at stopprice stop;
end;
end;
if marketposition= -1 then begin
profitprice= entryprice * (1 - ptarget/100);
stopprice= entryprice * (1 + stopl/100);
buy to cover next bar at profitprice limit;
buy to cover next bar at stopprice stop;
end;

{File:DAX.txt Index:6 Index Date:20050223 PL:15.63% PS:
84.38% Trades:32 CL:1}
{SHORT, %, TARGET: 2, STOP: 4, ENTRY PRICE: OPEN, DELAY: 0}
input: ptarget (2), stopl (4);
variables: profitprice (0), stopprice (0);
if c[4] > c[2] AND c[2] > c[3] AND c[3] > c[1] AND c[1] >
c[0] then begin
```

```
Sell Short Next Bar at open;
if Marketposition = 0 then begin
profitprice = O of tomorrow * (1-ptarget/100);
stopprice = O of tomorrow * (1+stopl/100);
buy to cover next bar at profitprice limit;
buy to cover next bar at stopprice stop;
end;
end;
if marketposition= -1 then begin
profitprice= entryprice * (1 - ptarget/100);
stopprice= entryprice * (1 + stopl/100);
buy to cover next bar at profitprice limit;
buy to cover next bar at stopprice stop;
end;


{File:DAX.txt Index:4 Index Date:20050202 PL:80.00% PS:
20.00% Trades:30 CL:1}
{LONG, %, TARGET: 2, STOP: 4, ENTRY PRICE: OPEN, DELAY: 0}
input: ptarget (2), stopl (4);
variables: profitprice (0), stopprice (0);
if h[0] > h[1] AND h[1] > l[0] AND l[0] > h[2] AND h[2] >
l[1] AND l[1] > h[3] AND h[3] > l[2] AND l[2] > l[3] then
begin
Buy Next Bar at open;
if Marketposition = 0 then begin
profitprice = O of tomorrow * (1+ptarget/100);
stopprice = O of tomorrow * (1-stopl/100);
sell next bar at profitprice limit;
sell next bar at stopprice stop;
end;
end;
if marketposition= 1 then begin
profitprice= entryprice * (1 + ptarget/100);
stopprice= entryprice * (1 - stopl/100);
sell next bar at profitprice limit;
sell next bar at stopprice stop;
end;
```

3. Wealth-Lab Script Wealth-Lab code for selected DAX patterns. Wealth-Lab is a trademark of WL Systems, Inc.

```
// File:DAX.txt Index:11 Index Date:20050121 PL:68.42% PS:
31.58% Trades:38 CL:3
// LONG, %, TARGET: 3, STOP: 3, ENTRY PRICE: OPEN, DELAY: 0
var Bar: integer;
SetAutoStopMode (#AsPercent);
```

```
InstallProfitTarget (3);
InstallStopLoss (3);
for Bar:= 12 to BarCount - 1 do
begin
if not LastPositionActive then begin
if (PriceLow (Bar-2) > PriceHigh (Bar-0)) AND (PriceHigh
(Bar-0) > PriceLow (Bar-3)) AND (PriceLow (Bar-3) >
PriceLow (Bar-1)) then
BuyAtMarket (Bar+1, 'Open');
end
else
ApplyAutoStops (Bar);
end;

// File:DAX.txt Index:10 Index Date:20050331 PL:32.26% PS:
67.74% Trades:31 CL:2
// SHORT, %, TARGET: 3, STOP: 3, ENTRY PRICE: OPEN, DELAY: 0
var Bar: integer;
SetAutoStopMode (#AsPercent);
InstallProfitTarget (3);
InstallStopLoss (3);
for Bar:= 12 to BarCount - 1 do
begin
if not LastPositionActive then begin
if (PriceHigh (Bar-0) > PriceHigh (Bar-1)) AND (PriceHigh
(Bar-1) > PriceHigh (Bar-2)) AND (PriceHigh (Bar-2) >
PriceClose (Bar-0)) AND (PriceClose (Bar-0) > PriceLow
(Bar-0)) AND (PriceLow (Bar-0) > PriceLow (Bar-1)) AND
(PriceLow (Bar-1) > PriceLow (Bar-2)) then
ShortAtMarket (Bar + 1, 'Open');
end
else
ApplyAutoStops (Bar);
end;

// File:DAX.txt Index:6 Index Date:20050223 PL:15.63% PS:
84.38% Trades:32 CL:1
// SHORT, %, TARGET: 2, STOP: 4, ENTRY PRICE: OPEN, DELAY: 0
var Bar: integer;
SetAutoStopMode (#AsPercent);
InstallProfitTarget (2);
InstallStopLoss (4);
for Bar:= 12 to BarCount - 1 do
begin
if not LastPositionActive then begin
if (PriceClose (Bar-4) > PriceClose (Bar-2)) AND
```

```
(PriceClose (Bar-2) > PriceClose (Bar-3)) AND (PriceClose
(Bar-3) > PriceClose (Bar-1)) AND (PriceClose (Bar-1) >
PriceClose (Bar-0)) then
ShortAtMarket (Bar + 1, 'Open');
end
else
ApplyAutoStops (Bar);
end;


// File:DAX.txt Index:4 Index Date:20050202 PL:80.00% PS:
20.00% Trades:30 CL:1
// LONG, %, TARGET: 2, STOP: 4, ENTRY PRICE: OPEN, DELAY: 0
var Bar: integer;
SetAutoStopMode (#AsPercent);
InstallProfitTarget (2);
InstallStopLoss (4);
for Bar:= 12 to BarCount - 1 do
begin
if not LastPositionActive then begin
if (PriceHigh (Bar-0) > PriceHigh (Bar-1)) AND (PriceHigh
(Bar-1) > PriceLow (Bar-0)) AND (PriceLow (Bar-0) >
PriceHigh (Bar-2)) AND (PriceHigh (Bar-2) > PriceLow
(Bar-1)) AND (PriceLow (Bar-1) > PriceHigh (Bar-3)) AND
(PriceHigh (Bar-3) > PriceLow (Bar-2)) AND (PriceLow
(Bar-2) > PriceLow (Bar-3)) then
BuyAtMarket (Bar+1, 'Open');
end
else
ApplyAutoStops (Bar);
end;
```

FTSE Patterns

1. Metastock Formula Code Metastock code for selected FTSE patterns. Metastock® is a registered trademark of Equis International, a Reuters company.

```
{File:FTSE.txt Index:3 Index Date:20040712 PL:15.71% PS:
84.29% Trades:70 CL:2}
{SHORT, %, TARGET: 2, STOP: 4, ENTRY PRICE: OPEN, DELAY: 1}
(Ref (h,-1) > Ref (h,0)) AND (Ref (h,0) > Ref (h,-2)) AND
(Ref (h,-2) > Ref (l,-1)) AND (Ref (l,-1) > Ref (l,0)) AND
(Ref (l,0) > Ref (l,-2))

{File:FTSE.txt Index:12 Index Date:20041015 PL:81.97% PS:
18.03% Trades:61 CL:2}
```

{LONG, %, TARGET: 2, STOP: 4, ENTRY PRICE: OPEN, DELAY: 1}
(Ref (l,-4) > Ref (h,0)) AND (Ref (h,0) > Ref (l,-3)) AND
(Ref (l,-3) > Ref (l,-2)) AND (Ref (l,-2) > Ref (l,-1))

{File:FTSE.txt Index:10 Index Date:20040730 PL:19.64% PS:
80.36% Trades:56 CL:1}
{SHORT, %, TARGET: 2, STOP: 4, ENTRY PRICE: OPEN, DELAY: 2}
(Ref (h,0) > Ref (h,-1)) AND (Ref (h,-1) > Ref (c,0)) AND
(Ref (c,0) > Ref (l,0)) AND (Ref (l,0) > Ref (h,-2)) AND
(Ref (h,-2) > Ref (l,-1)) AND (Ref (l,-1) > Ref (l,-2))

{File:FTSE.txt Index:5 Index Date:20040922 PL:18.18% PS:
81.82% Trades:55 CL:2}
{SHORT, %, TARGET: 2, STOP: 4, ENTRY PRICE: OPEN, DELAY: 1}
(Ref (c,-1) > Ref (c,0)) AND (Ref (c,0) > Ref (c,-3)) AND
(Ref (c,-3) > Ref (c,-2))

{File:FTSE.txt Index:5 Index Date:20041019 PL:15.38% PS:
84.62% Trades:52 CL:1}
{SHORT, %, TARGET: 2, STOP: 4, ENTRY PRICE: OPEN, DELAY: 3}
(Ref (c,0) > Ref (c,-3)) AND (Ref (c,-3) > Ref (c,-2)) AND
(Ref (c,-2) > Ref (c,-1))

{File:FTSE.txt Index:12 Index Date:20040917 PL:19.61% PS:
80.39% Trades:51 CL:2}
{SHORT, %, TARGET: 2, STOP: 4, ENTRY PRICE: OPEN, DELAY: 3}
(Ref (h,0) > Ref (l,-4)) AND (Ref (l,-4) > Ref (l,-1)) AND
(Ref (l,-1) > Ref (l,-2)) AND (Ref (l,-2) > Ref (l,-3))

{File:FTSE.txt Index:3 Index Date:20041007 PL:83.67% PS:
16.33% Trades:49 CL:2}
{LONG, %, TARGET: 2, STOP: 4, ENTRY PRICE: OPEN, DELAY: 4}
(Ref (h,0) > Ref (h,-1)) AND (Ref (h,-1) > Ref (h,-2)) AND
(Ref (h,-2) > Ref (l,-1)) AND (Ref (l,-1) > Ref (l,0)) AND
(Ref (l,0) > Ref (l,-2))

{File:FTSE.txt Index:12 Index Date:20040930 PL:81.40% PS:
18.60% Trades:43 CL:3}
{LONG, %, TARGET: 2, STOP: 4, ENTRY PRICE: OPEN, DELAY: 4}
(Ref (h,0) > Ref (l,-1)) AND (Ref (l,-1) > Ref (l,-4)) AND
(Ref (l,-4) > Ref (l,-3)) AND (Ref (l,-3) > Ref (l,-2))

{File:FTSE.txt Index:12 Index Date:20040728 PL:16.28% PS:
83.72% Trades:43 CL:1}
{SHORT, %, TARGET: 2, STOP: 4, ENTRY PRICE: OPEN, DELAY: 3}
(Ref (h,0) > Ref (l,-3)) AND (Ref (l,-3) > Ref (l,-4)) AND
(Ref (l,-4) > Ref (l,-1)) AND (Ref (l,-1) > Ref (l,-2))

```
{File:FTSE.txt Index:3 Index Date:20040804 PL:80.95% PS:
19.05% Trades:42 CL:2}
{LONG, %, TARGET: 2, STOP: 4, ENTRY PRICE: OPEN, DELAY: 4}
(Ref (h,-1) > Ref (h,0)) AND (Ref (h,0) > Ref (h,-2)) AND
(Ref (h,-2) > Ref (l,-1)) AND (Ref (l,-1) > Ref (l,-2)) AND
(Ref (l,-2) > Ref (l,0))
```

2. EasyLanguage Code EasyLanguage® code for selected FTSE patterns. EasyLanguage® is a registered trademark of TradeStation Technologies, Inc.

```
{File:FTSE.txt Index:3 Index Date:20040712 PL:15.71% PS:
84.29% Trades:70 CL:2}
{SHORT, %, TARGET: 2, STOP: 4, ENTRY PRICE: OPEN, DELAY: 0}
input: ptarget (2), stopl (4);
variables: profitprice (0), stopprice (0);
if h[1] > h[0] AND h[0] > h[2] AND h[2] > l[1] AND l[1] >
l[0] AND l[0] > l[2] then begin
Sell Short Next Bar at open;
if Marketposition = 0 then begin
profitprice = O of tomorrow * (1-ptarget/100);
stopprice = O of tomorrow * (1+stopl/100);
buy to cover next bar at profitprice limit;
buy to cover next bar at stopprice stop;
end;
end;
if marketposition= -1 then begin
profitprice= entryprice * (1 - ptarget/100);
stopprice= entryprice * (1 + stopl/100);
buy to cover next bar at profitprice limit;
buy to cover next bar at stopprice stop;
end;

{File:FTSE.txt Index:12 Index Date:20041015 PL:81.97% PS:
18.03% Trades:61 CL:2}
{LONG, %, TARGET: 2, STOP: 4, ENTRY PRICE: OPEN, DELAY: 0}
input: ptarget (2), stopl (4);
variables: profitprice (0), stopprice (0);
if l[4] > h[0] AND h[0] > l[3] AND l[3] > l[2] AND l[2] >
l[1] then begin
Buy Next Bar at open;
if Marketposition = 0 then begin
profitprice = O of tomorrow * (1+ptarget/100);
stopprice = O of tomorrow * (1-stopl/100);
sell next bar at profitprice limit;
sell next bar at stopprice stop;
```

170

```
end;
end;
if marketposition= 1 then begin
profitprice= entryprice * (1 + ptarget/100);
stopprice= entryprice * (1 - stopl/100);
sell next bar at profitprice limit;
sell next bar at stopprice stop;
end;

{File:FTSE.txt Index:10 Index Date:20040730 PL:19.64% PS:
80.36% Trades:56 CL:1}
{SHORT, %, TARGET: 2, STOP: 4, ENTRY PRICE: OPEN, DELAY: 1}
input: ptarget (2), stopl (4);
variables: profitprice (0), stopprice (0);
if h[1] > h[2] AND h[2] > c[1] AND c[1] > l[1] AND l[1] >
h[3] AND h[3] > l[2] AND l[2] > l[3] then begin
Sell Short Next Bar at open;
if Marketposition = 0 then begin
profitprice = O of tomorrow * (1-ptarget/100);
stopprice = O of tomorrow * (1+stopl/100);
buy to cover next bar at profitprice limit;
buy to cover next bar at stopprice stop;
end;
end;
if marketposition= -1 then begin
profitprice= entryprice * (1 - ptarget/100);
stopprice= entryprice * (1 + stopl/100);
buy to cover next bar at profitprice limit;
buy to cover next bar at stopprice stop;
end;

{File:FTSE.txt Index:5 Index Date:20040922 PL:18.18% PS:
81.82% Trades:55 CL:2}
{SHORT, %, TARGET: 2, STOP: 4, ENTRY PRICE: OPEN, DELAY: 0}
input: ptarget (2), stopl (4);
variables: profitprice (0), stopprice (0);
if c[1] > c[0] AND c[0] > c[3] AND c[3] > c[2] then begin
Sell Short Next Bar at open;
if Marketposition = 0 then begin
profitprice = O of tomorrow * (1-ptarget/100);
stopprice = O of tomorrow * (1+stopl/100);
buy to cover next bar at profitprice limit;
buy to cover next bar at stopprice stop;
end;
end;
if marketposition= -1 then begin
profitprice= entryprice * (1 - ptarget/100);
```

```
stopprice= entryprice * (1 + stopl/100);
buy to cover next bar at profitprice limit;
buy to cover next bar at stopprice stop;
end;

{File:FTSE.txt Index:5 Index Date:20041019 PL:15.38% PS:
84.62% Trades:52 CL:1}
{SHORT, %, TARGET: 2, STOP: 4, ENTRY PRICE: OPEN, DELAY: 2}
input: ptarget (2), stopl (4);
variables: profitprice (0), stopprice (0);
if c[2] > c[5] AND c[5] > c[4] AND c[4] > c[3] then begin
Sell Short Next Bar at open;
if Marketposition = 0 then begin
profitprice = O of tomorrow * (1-ptarget/100);
stopprice = O of tomorrow * (1+stopl/100);
buy to cover next bar at profitprice limit;
buy to cover next bar at stopprice stop;
end;
end;
if marketposition= -1 then begin
profitprice= entryprice * (1 - ptarget/100);
stopprice= entryprice * (1 + stopl/100);
buy to cover next bar at profitprice limit;
buy to cover next bar at stopprice stop;
end;

{File:FTSE.txt Index:12 Index Date:20040917 PL:19.61% PS:
80.39% Trades:51 CL:2}
{SHORT, %, TARGET: 2, STOP: 4, ENTRY PRICE: OPEN, DELAY: 2}
input: ptarget (2), stopl (4);
variables: profitprice (0), stopprice (0);
if h[2] > l[6] AND l[6] > l[3] AND l[3] > l[4] AND l[4] >
l[5] then begin
Sell Short Next Bar at open;
if Marketposition = 0 then begin
profitprice = O of tomorrow * (1-ptarget/100);
stopprice = O of tomorrow * (1+stopl/100);
buy to cover next bar at profitprice limit;
buy to cover next bar at stopprice stop;
end;
end;
if marketposition= -1 then begin
profitprice= entryprice * (1 - ptarget/100);
stopprice= entryprice * (1 + stopl/100);
buy to cover next bar at profitprice limit;
buy to cover next bar at stopprice stop;
end;
```

```
{File:FTSE.txt Index:3 Index Date:20041007 PL:83.67% PS:
16.33% Trades:49 CL:2}
{LONG, %, TARGET: 2, STOP: 4, ENTRY PRICE: OPEN, DELAY: 3}
input: ptarget (2), stopl (4);
variables: profitprice (0), stopprice (0);
if h[3] > h[4] AND h[4] > h[5] AND h[5] > l[4] AND l[4] >
l[3] AND l[3] > l[5] then begin
Buy Next Bar at open;
if Marketposition = 0 then begin
profitprice = O of tomorrow * (1+ptarget/100);
stopprice = O of tomorrow * (1-stopl/100);
sell next bar at profitprice limit;
sell next bar at stopprice stop;
end;
end;
if marketposition= 1 then begin
profitprice= entryprice * (1 + ptarget/100);
stopprice= entryprice * (1 - stopl/100);
sell next bar at profitprice limit;
sell next bar at stopprice stop;
end;

{File:FTSE.txt Index:12 Index Date:20040930 PL:81.40% PS:
18.60% Trades:43 CL:3}
{LONG, %, TARGET: 2, STOP: 4, ENTRY PRICE: OPEN, DELAY: 3}
input: ptarget (2), stopl (4);
variables: profitprice (0), stopprice (0);
if h[3] > l[4] AND l[4] > l[7] AND l[7] > l[6] AND l[6] >
l[5] then begin
Buy Next Bar at open;
if Marketposition = 0 then begin
profitprice = O of tomorrow * (1+ptarget/100);
stopprice = O of tomorrow * (1-stopl/100);
sell next bar at profitprice limit;
sell next bar at stopprice stop;
end;
end;
if marketposition= 1 then begin
profitprice= entryprice * (1 + ptarget/100);
stopprice= entryprice * (1 - stopl/100);
sell next bar at profitprice limit;
sell next bar at stopprice stop;
end;

{File:FTSE.txt Index:12 Index Date:20040728 PL:16.28% PS:
83.72% Trades:43 CL:1}
{SHORT, %, TARGET: 2, STOP: 4, ENTRY PRICE: OPEN, DELAY: 2}
```

```
input: ptarget (2), stopl (4);
variables: profitprice (0), stopprice (0);
if h[2] > l[5] AND l[5] > l[6] AND l[6] > l[3] AND l[3] >
l[4] then begin
Sell Short Next Bar at open;
if Marketposition = 0 then begin
profitprice = O of tomorrow * (1-ptarget/100);
stopprice = O of tomorrow * (1+stopl/100);
buy to cover next bar at profitprice limit;
buy to cover next bar at stopprice stop;
end;
end;
if marketposition= -1 then begin
profitprice= entryprice * (1 - ptarget/100);
stopprice= entryprice * (1 + stopl/100);
buy to cover next bar at profitprice limit;
buy to cover next bar at stopprice stop;
end;

{File:FTSE.txt Index:3 Index Date:20040804 PL:80.95% PS:
19.05% Trades:42 CL:2}
{LONG, %, TARGET: 2, STOP: 4, ENTRY PRICE: OPEN, DELAY: 3}
input: ptarget (2), stopl (4);
variables: profitprice (0), stopprice (0);
if h[4] > h[3] AND h[3] > h[5] AND h[5] > l[4] AND l[4] >
l[5] AND l[5] > l[3] then begin
Buy Next Bar at open;
if Marketposition = 0 then begin
profitprice = O of tomorrow * (1+ptarget/100);
stopprice = O of tomorrow * (1-stopl/100);
sell next bar at profitprice limit;
sell next bar at stopprice stop;
end;
end;
if marketposition= 1 then begin
profitprice= entryprice * (1 + ptarget/100);
stopprice= entryprice * (1 - stopl/100);
sell next bar at profitprice limit;
sell next bar at stopprice stop;
end;
```

3. Wealth-Lab Script Wealth-Lab code for selected FTSE patterns. Wealth-Lab is a trademark of WL Systems, Inc.

```
// File:FTSE.txt Index:3 Index Date:20040712 PL:15.71% PS:
84.29% Trades:70 CL:2
```

```
// SHORT, %, TARGET: 2, STOP: 4, ENTRY PRICE: OPEN, DELAY: 0
var Bar: integer;
SetAutoStopMode (#AsPercent);
InstallProfitTarget (2);
InstallStopLoss (4);
for Bar:= 12 to BarCount - 1 do
begin
if not LastPositionActive then begin
if (PriceHigh (Bar-1) > PriceHigh (Bar-0)) AND (PriceHigh
(Bar-0) > PriceHigh (Bar-2)) AND (PriceHigh (Bar-2) >
PriceLow (Bar-1)) AND (PriceLow (Bar-1) > PriceLow (Bar-0))
AND (PriceLow (Bar-0) > PriceLow (Bar-2)) then
ShortAtMarket (Bar + 1, 'Open');
end
else
ApplyAutoStops (Bar);
end;


// File:FTSE.txt Index:12 Index Date:20041015 PL:81.97% PS:
18.03% Trades:61 CL:2
// LONG, %, TARGET: 2, STOP: 4, ENTRY PRICE: OPEN, DELAY: 0
var Bar: integer;
SetAutoStopMode (#AsPercent);
InstallProfitTarget (2);
InstallStopLoss (4);
for Bar:= 12 to BarCount - 1 do
begin
if not LastPositionActive then begin
if (PriceLow (Bar-4) > PriceHigh (Bar-0)) AND (PriceHigh
(Bar-0) > PriceLow (Bar-3)) AND (PriceLow (Bar-3) >
PriceLow (Bar-2)) AND (PriceLow (Bar-2) > PriceLow (Bar-1))
then
BuyAtMarket (Bar+1, 'Open');
end
else
ApplyAutoStops (Bar);
end;


// File:FTSE.txt Index:10 Index Date:20040730 PL:19.64% PS:
80.36% Trades:56 CL:1
// SHORT, %, TARGET: 2, STOP: 4, ENTRY PRICE: OPEN, DELAY: 1
var Bar: integer;
SetAutoStopMode (#AsPercent);
InstallProfitTarget (2);
InstallStopLoss (4);
for Bar:= 12 to BarCount - 1 do
```

```
begin
if not LastPositionActive then begin
if (PriceHigh (Bar-1) > PriceHigh (Bar-2)) AND (PriceHigh
(Bar-2) > PriceClose (Bar-1)) AND (PriceClose (Bar-1) >
PriceLow (Bar-1)) AND (PriceLow (Bar-1) > PriceHigh
(Bar-3)) AND (PriceHigh (Bar-3) > PriceLow (Bar-2)) AND
(PriceLow (Bar-2) > PriceLow (Bar-3)) then
ShortAtMarket (Bar + 1, 'Open');
end
else
ApplyAutoStops (Bar);
end;


// File:FTSE.txt Index:5 Index Date:20040922 PL:18.18% PS:
81.82% Trades:55 CL:2
// SHORT, %, TARGET: 2, STOP: 4, ENTRY PRICE: OPEN, DELAY: 0
var Bar: integer;
SetAutoStopMode (#AsPercent);
InstallProfitTarget (2);
InstallStopLoss (4);
for Bar:= 12 to BarCount - 1 do
begin
if not LastPositionActive then begin
if (PriceClose (Bar-1) > PriceClose (Bar-0)) AND
(PriceClose (Bar-0) > PriceClose (Bar-3)) AND (PriceClose
(Bar-3) > PriceClose (Bar-2)) then
ShortAtMarket (Bar + 1, 'Open');
end
else
ApplyAutoStops (Bar);
end;


// File:FTSE.txt Index:5 Index Date:20041019 PL:15.38% PS:
84.62% Trades:52 CL:1
// SHORT, %, TARGET: 2, STOP: 4, ENTRY PRICE: OPEN, DELAY: 2
var Bar: integer;
SetAutoStopMode (#AsPercent);
InstallProfitTarget (2);
InstallStopLoss (4);
for Bar:= 12 to BarCount - 1 do
begin
if not LastPositionActive then begin
if (PriceClose (Bar-2) > PriceClose (Bar-5)) AND
(PriceClose (Bar-5) > PriceClose (Bar-4)) AND (PriceClose
(Bar-4) > PriceClose (Bar-3)) then
ShortAtMarket (Bar + 1, 'Open');
```

```
end
else
ApplyAutoStops (Bar);
end;

// File:FTSE.txt Index:12 Index Date:20040917 PL:19.61% PS:
80.39% Trades:51 CL:2
// SHORT, %, TARGET: 2, STOP: 4, ENTRY PRICE: OPEN, DELAY: 2
var Bar: integer;
SetAutoStopMode (#AsPercent);
InstallProfitTarget (2);
InstallStopLoss (4);
for Bar:= 12 to BarCount - 1 do
begin
if not LastPositionActive then begin
if (PriceHigh (Bar-2) > PriceLow (Bar-6)) AND (PriceLow
(Bar-6) > PriceLow (Bar-3)) AND (PriceLow (Bar-3) >
PriceLow (Bar-4)) AND (PriceLow (Bar-4) > PriceLow (Bar-5))
then
ShortAtMarket (Bar + 1, 'Open');
end
else
ApplyAutoStops (Bar);
end;

// File:FTSE.txt Index:3 Index Date:20041007 PL:83.67% PS:
16.33% Trades:49 CL:2
// LONG, %, TARGET: 2, STOP: 4, ENTRY PRICE: OPEN, DELAY: 3
var Bar: integer;
SetAutoStopMode (#AsPercent);
InstallProfitTarget (2);
InstallStopLoss (4);
for Bar:= 12 to BarCount - 1 do
begin
if not LastPositionActive then begin
if (PriceHigh (Bar-3) > PriceHigh (Bar-4)) AND (PriceHigh
(Bar-4) > PriceHigh (Bar-5)) AND (PriceHigh (Bar-5) >
PriceLow (Bar-4)) AND (PriceLow (Bar-4) > PriceLow (Bar-3))
AND (PriceLow (Bar-3) > PriceLow (Bar-5)) then
BuyAtMarket (Bar+1, 'Open');
end
else
ApplyAutoStops (Bar);
end;

// File:FTSE.txt Index:12 Index Date:20040930 PL:81.40% PS:
18.60% Trades:43 CL:3
```

```
// LONG, %, TARGET: 2, STOP: 4, ENTRY PRICE: OPEN, DELAY: 3
var Bar: integer;
SetAutoStopMode (#AsPercent);
InstallProfitTarget (2);
InstallStopLoss (4);
for Bar:= 12 to BarCount - 1 do
begin
if not LastPositionActive then begin
if (PriceHigh (Bar-3) > PriceLow (Bar-4)) AND (PriceLow
(Bar-4) > PriceLow (Bar-7)) AND (PriceLow (Bar-7) >
PriceLow (Bar-6)) AND (PriceLow (Bar-6) > PriceLow (Bar-5))
then
BuyAtMarket (Bar+1, 'Open');
end
else
ApplyAutoStops (Bar);
end;


// File:FTSE.txt Index:12 Index Date:20040728 PL:16.28% PS:
83.72% Trades:43 CL:1
// SHORT, %, TARGET: 2, STOP: 4, ENTRY PRICE: OPEN, DELAY: 2
var Bar: integer;
SetAutoStopMode (#AsPercent);
InstallProfitTarget (2);
InstallStopLoss (4);
for Bar:= 12 to BarCount - 1 do
begin
if not LastPositionActive then begin
if (PriceHigh (Bar-2) > PriceLow (Bar-5)) AND (PriceLow
(Bar-5) > PriceLow (Bar-6)) AND (PriceLow (Bar-6) >
PriceLow (Bar-3)) AND (PriceLow (Bar-3) > PriceLow (Bar-4))
then
ShortAtMarket (Bar + 1, 'Open');
end
else
ApplyAutoStops (Bar);
end;


// File:FTSE.txt Index:3 Index Date:20040804 PL:80.95% PS:
19.05% Trades:42 CL:2
// LONG, %, TARGET: 2, STOP: 4, ENTRY PRICE: OPEN, DELAY: 3
var Bar: integer;
SetAutoStopMode (#AsPercent);
InstallProfitTarget (2);
InstallStopLoss (4);
for Bar:= 12 to BarCount - 1 do
begin
```

```
if not LastPositionActive then begin
if (PriceHigh (Bar-4) > PriceHigh (Bar-3)) AND (PriceHigh
(Bar-3) > PriceHigh (Bar-5)) AND (PriceHigh (Bar-5) >
PriceLow (Bar-4)) AND (PriceLow (Bar-4) > PriceLow (Bar-5))
AND (PriceLow (Bar-5) > PriceLow (Bar-3)) then
BuyAtMarket (Bar+1, 'Open');
end
else
ApplyAutoStops (Bar);
end;
```

References

BOOKS

Harris, M. *Stock Trading Techniques Based on Price Patterns*. Traders Press, Inc., 2001.

Harris, M. *Short-Term Trading with Price Patterns*. Traders Press, Inc., 2000.

Papoulis, A. *Probability, Random Variables, and Stochastic Processes*. New York: McGraw-Hill, 1965, pp. 57–61.

ARTICLES BY MICHAEL HARRIS

"Trading Probabilities," *Active Trader*, March 2001, p. 76.

"Keeping It Simple," *Active Trader*, September 2001, p. 82.

"Beyond Strategy Testing," *Active Trader*, March 2002, p. 70.

"Facing the Facts of Risk and Money Management," *Active Trader*, May 2002, p. 54.

"Simple but Effective," *Active Trader*, June 2002, p. 64.

"Price Pattern Autopilot," *Active Trader*, September 2002, p. 70.

"The Profitability Rule," *Stocks & Commodities*, September 2002, p. 30.

"When It Pays to Wait," *Active Trader*, February 2003, p. 48.

"Trend Trading with Short-term Price Patterns," *Active Trader*, June 2003, p. 31.

"Testing for Profitable Short-term Price Patterns," *Traders'*, January 2005.

"Using a Trade Input Delay," *Traders'*, March 2005.

"Price Patterns Surviving the Test of Time," *Traders'*, May 2005.

SOFTWARE

Price Pattern Automatic Discovery

APS Automatic Pattern Search by Tradingpatterns.com,
http://www.tradingpatterns.com.

Charting and Back-Testing

Metastock by Equis International, a Reuters company, http://www.equis.com.

TradeStation by TradeStation Technologies, http://www.tradestation.com.

Wealth-Lab by WL Systems, Inc., http://www.wealth-lab.com.

About the CD-ROM

INTRODUCTION

This appendix provides you with information on the contents of the CD that accompanies this book. For the latest and greatest information, please refer to the ReadMe file located at the root of the CD.

System Requirements

- A computer with a processor running at 120 Mhz or faster
- At least 32 MB of total RAM installed on your computer; for best performance, we recommend at least 64 MB
- A CD-ROM drive

USING THE CD WITH WINDOWS

To install the items from the CD to your hard drive, follow these steps:

1. Insert the CD into your computer's CD-ROM drive.
2. The CD-ROM interface will appear. The interface provides a simple point-and-click way to explore the contents of the CD.

   If the opening screen of the CD-ROM does not appear automatically, follow these steps to access the CD:
3. Click the Start button on the left end of the taskbar and then choose Run from the menu that pops up.
4. In the dialog box that appears, type *d:\start.exe*. (If your CD-ROM drive is not drive d, fill in the appropriate letter in place of *d*.) This brings up the CD Interface described in the preceding set of steps.

WHAT'S ON THE CD

The following sections provide a summary of the software and other materials you'll find on the CD.

Content

Any material from the book, including forms, slides, and lesson plans if available, are in the folder named "Content."

Codes:

File: codes for selected price patterns.pdf

This CD contains the codes for selected price patterns, which are listed in the Appendix section of the book. As these codes are in a pdf file, opening the file requires Adobe Reader.

Readers of the book who would like to test the code can copy and paste it from this pdf file into Metastock, Tradestation, or Wealth-lab instead of manually reproducing it.

Software:

File: apsdv49.exe

The file **apsdv49.exe** is for installing the demo version of APS Automatic Pattern Search v4.9, the program used to generate the codes for the price patterns in the Appendix of the book. Readers can use the program to study how the values of various parameters affect synthesis of trading systems based on price patterns, the method of system development discussed in Chapter 7 of the book. Also, the following two support files are included for the demo users and can be opened with NotePad.:

Software support files:

Demo Installation Instructions.txt: This file contains instructions about installing the demo version of Automatic Pattern Search on your computer and lists the hardware/software requirements and Windows Vista Compatibility issues.

Tips for a quick start.txt: This file contains tips for using Automatic Pattern Search, like setting up a search or a scan of workspaces. More information can be found in the program manual that is included in the program installation in the form of a help file.

Data files:

Sample historical data files are included that can be used by APS Automatic Pattern Search demo version to determine how the choice of the value of parameters, such as profitability and number of historical trades, affect price pattern synthesis, the method of system development described in Chapter 7.

Applications

The following applications are on the CD:

> **Adobe Reader.** Adobe Reader is a freeware application for viewing files in the Adobe Portable Document format.

Trial, demo, or evaluation versions are usually limited either by time or functionality (such as being unable to save projects). Some trial versions are very sensitive to system date changes. If you alter your computer's date, the programs will "time out" and no longer be functional.

CUSTOMER CARE

If you have trouble with the CD-ROM, please call the Wiley Product Technical Support phone number at (800) 762-2974. Outside the United States, call 1(317) 572-3994. You can also contact Wiley Product Technical Support at **http://support.wiley.com**. John Wiley & Sons will provide technical support only for installation and other general quality control items. For technical support on the applications themselves, consult the program's vendor or author.

To place additional orders or to request information about other Wiley products, please call (877) 762-2974.

CUSTOMER NOTE: IF THIS BOOK IS ACCOMPANIED BY SOFT-WARE, PLEASE READ THE FOLLOWING BEFORE OPENING THE PACKAGE.

This software contains files to help you utilize the models described in the accompanying book. By opening the package, you are agreeing to be bound by the following agreement:

This software product is protected by copyright and all rights are reserved by the author, John Wiley & Sons, Inc., or their licensors. You are licensed to use this software on a single computer. Copying the software

Index